Quick *and* easy TOPIARY *and* green SCULPTURE

Quick *and* easy TOPIARY *and* green SCULPTURE

STOREY BOOKS

Schoolhouse Road
Pownal, Vermont 05261

The mission of Storey Communications is to serve our customers by publishing practical information that encourages personal independence in harmony with the environment.

United States edition published in 1996 by Storey Communications, Inc., Schoolhouse Road, Pownal, Vermont 05261.

Senior Editor ✳ *Sian Parkhouse*
Art Editor ✳ *Anne Fisher*
Designer ✳ *Debbie Mole*
Copy Editor ✳ *Louisa McDonnell*
Picture Researcher ✳ *Jo Carlill*
Picture Manager ✳ *Giulia Hetherington*
Photographers ✳ *Paul Forrester, Colin Bowling*
Illustrator ✳ *Elisabeth Dowle*
Art Director ✳ *Moira Clinch*
Editorial Director ✳ *Mark Dartford*
Storey Communications Editor ✳ *Gwen W. Steege*

This book was designed and produced by
Quarto Publishing plc ✳ *6 Blundell Street* ✳ *London N7 9BH*

Storey Books are available for special premium and promotional uses and for customized editions. For further information, please call Storey's Custom Publishing Department at 1-800-793-9396.

Typeset by *Central Southern Typesetters, Eastbourne*
Manufactured by *J. Film Process, Singapore (Pte) Ltd*
Printed in China by Leefung-Asco Printers Ltd

10 9 8 7 6 5 4 3 2

Library of Congress Cataloging-in-Publication Data

Hendy, Jenny. 1961–
Quick and easy topiary and green sculpture / Jenny Hendy.
p. cm.

ISBN 0-88266-920-6 (pb. : alk. paper)
1. Topiary work. 2. Ornamental climbing plants—Training.
I. Title.
SB463.H46 1996   95-22905
715′.1—dc20   CIP

CONTENTS

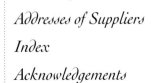

LEFT
The deliciously scented heliotropes make excellent mini standards for the sun room or summer patio. They come in various shades, of purple, pink and also white like this variety 'White Lady.'

RIGHT
This amazing menagerie at Portsmouth, Rhode Island, took many years to create. Small-scale versions can be made in a fraction of the time.

INTRODUCTION

LEFT
Passersby must do a double take when they see what's guarding the entrance to this traditional thatched cottage! Let your imagination run wild and create your own fantasy landscape.

LEFT
Formal box spirals, cones, and spheres line this avenue at Bourton House in Gloucestershire, England.

BELOW
Sitting on the edge of a herb bed, this whimsical figure made from trained box appears to be taking a well-earned rest from her gardening.

As you leaf through the pages of this book, you'll discover that topiary, or green sculpture, is well within the reach of even a novice gardener. You really do not need any previous experience, and with easy-to-follow, step-by-step instructions, even an apparently complex design becomes simplicity itself.

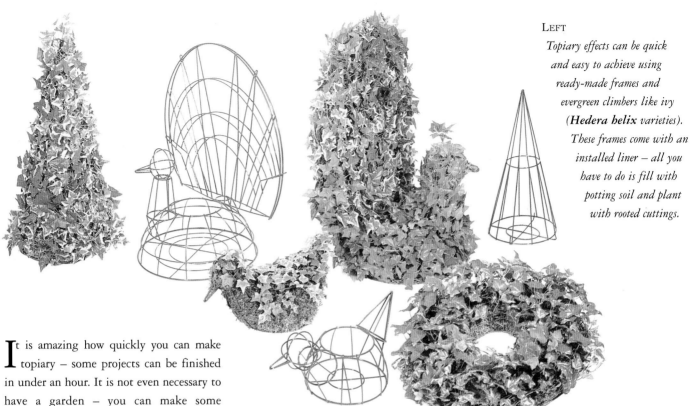

LEFT
*Topiary effects can be quick
and easy to achieve using
ready-made frames and
evergreen climbers like ivy
(**Hedera helix** varieties).
These frames come with an
installed liner – all you
have to do is fill with
potting soil and plant
with rooted cuttings.*

It is amazing how quickly you can make topiary – some projects can be finished in under an hour. It is not even necessary to have a garden – you can make some wonderful creations with house plants.

Although it is possible to buy ready-trained topiary, it is so much more fun and satisfying, as well as a lot less expensive, to make your own. Green sculptures make striking ornaments for garden, sun room, or home and, of course, delightful gifts for friends and relatives. Make them in whatever style or mood you prefer: formal or informal, quirky or imposing.

There is no doubt that a well-maintained topiary sculpture adds a touch of formality, grace, and elegance to the garden scene. Because of its sculptural qualities, most topiary associates well with hard landscaping – bricks and paving – and makes eye-catching decoration for a patio, terrace or balcony. Just as with any other garden ornament, topiary can be used to create a focal point or to emphasize a particular feature. Create symmetry using a matching pair of green sculptures to bracket a door, gate, archway, flight of steps, or garden seat. Place a large piece of topiary at the end of a path or rectangular lawn, or use a series of identical green globes or cones in pots to outline a terrace or formal pool.

Topiary figures can also be used to add structure and height in the flower border and, on a small scale, you can use mini-lollipop standards in window boxes and troughs, surrounded by lower-growing plants. Any moveable pot-grown topiary can be brought indoors for temporary display. Try standing large pieces on the ground in front of a floor-length mirror to double the effect, and for a party or special celebration, dress up outdoor pots with broad satin bows.

The book is split into six main sections starting with **Making Frames** which guides you through the construction of a variety of easy shapes in wire ranging from hearts and stars to a sculptural 3-D head. **Planting Frames** illustrates how to cover these and other frames to make instant topiary using a

LEFT
Make your own garden furniture – golden privet is a quick-growing alternative to box and can be clipped into almost any shape!

RIGHT
Box and lavender topiary add architectural detail to this simply designed terrace garden at Preen Manor, Shropshire in England. Evergreen topiary like this adds greatly to the winter garden landscape.

RIGHT

Freshly clipped,
this box spiral is
transformed into a
living sculpture.
A pair of matching
spirals or cones
placed on either side
of a path would
make an elegant
gateway.

wide range of plants including climbers like scented jasmine and small-leafed ivies, shrubs such as exotic abutilon and aromatic rosemary, as well as creeping and ground-covering plants like *Ficus pumila* and mind-your-own-business (*Soleirolia soleirolii*). One of the main techniques described here simply involves winding stems around to cover the outline of a frame. If you use ivy, there's not even any need to tie the shoots in position.

Adapting Traditional Topiary shows how surprisingly quick and easy it can be to shape and style plants by clipping and

LEFT

These geometric figures create an almost surreal garden landscape.

ABOVE

*These clipped flowering standards are trained from **Leptospermum scoparium**, the New Zealand tea tree, which produces a profusion of pink or white flowers from early to mid summer.*

LEFT

*Wire frames are extremely versatile – virtually any design is possible. This little elephant frame is covered in golden creeping Jenny (**Lysimachia nummularia** 'Aurea') rooted into moist moss.*

training to create green sculpture using fast-growing alternatives to traditional subjects like yew, bay and holly. There are step-by-step guides to producing geometric shapes such as cones, corkscrews and spheres as well as a super fan-tailed peacock. The methods for making standards ranging from mini-lollipops, suitable for table-top decoration to full-sized specimens are also included in this section. Find out how to make luscious fruiting standards from grape vines and figs or an elegant weeping wisteria standard for the patio.

Caring for your Topiary includes

everything you need to know about how to keep green sculpture in tip-top condition through the year and offers special advice on how to protect your most delicate pieces during the winter. **The Directory of Shapes** follows with scores of ideas for topiary under the headings: geometric; animals and birds; and special occasions. Finally, at the back of the book, is the **Plant Directory**. This is an illustrated guide to more than 150 varieties of flowering and foliage plants, all of which can be used in one or other form of topiary.

MAKING FRAMES

Although there are a good number of ready-made frames on the market, they can be pretty expensive and you may not be able to find just what you are looking for. If that's the case, then the answer is to make your own. In this chapter, we look at the basic techniques of frame-making and give step-by-step instructions for making a range of simple 2-D and 3-D frames. The tools and materials are all uncomplicated and once you have had some

LEFT TO RIGHT

Topiary frames come in all shapes, size and materials, including wicker (center), antiqued galvanized wire (all frames left of center), copper-coated soft steel wire (first right), galvanized wire (second right), and plastic-coated wire (far right). If you can't find a design you like, why not make your own (see pages 16 to 23).

experience of construction, you should be able to design your own shapes using photographs and illustrations from books and magazines for inspiration. The key to success is simplicity. The bolder and less fussy the outline of the frame, the more effective it is likely to be when covered with plants.

LEFT
A simple frame made from bamboo canes and wire transforms a "leggy" rosemary specimen into a column of aromatic greenery.

Traditionally, wooden frames were used to train large topiary. These were not necessarily ornamental and the wood eventually rotted, by which time the plant was already shaped and could stand on its own. By contrast, highly architectural treillage obelisks were very much designed to be on display. Today, wood and other natural materials are used to produce frames. These can be just as striking as those made from metal and wire and are often a lot cheaper to construct.

Garden sculptures using woven willow stems are becoming very popular now and are relatively easy to construct. Provided they are solidly attached to the ground, there is no reason why they shouldn't be used in the same way as wire topiary frames, and covered with climbers.

Wicker frames will eventually rot, but cost little to make and are enormous fun to construct. You can build simple geometric shapes like cones or domes or more abstract

forms, birds and animals. All you need is a supply of long, straight, pliable stems – various kinds of willow are traditionally used, but for small frames, it's a good idea to utilize winter prunings from Forsythia, or colored-stemmed dogwoods like *Cornus Stolonifera* 'Flaviramea' or *Cornus alba* 'Sibirica.' Stem thinnings – from common bamboos such as *Fargesia nitida* (syn. *Arundinaria nitida*) and *F. murieliae* provide excellent construction material which is strong, pliable, and long-lasting.

If you use freshly-cut willow, this will often root in the ground over winter and sprout fresh green shoots in the spring which can be rubbed off or left to add interest to the topiary.

Simple geometric designs can also be made by constructing a wooden frame and filling the gaps with square or diamond trellis, either making your own using roofing lathes nailed or stapled together, or buying the ready-made variety and cutting to size. One idea would be to make square trellis pillars for a wooden fence, or for either side of a doorway, and grow plants up through or over them depending on how

formal an effect is required. A wooden obelisk made in a similar fashion and stood either on the ground or in a square container such as a Versailles planter, would also be easy to construct.

Bamboo is a very versatile and easily shaped material, and you can buy several different lengths and thicknesses of cane depending on how big a construction you are building. When used in conjunction with wire, which can be bent, there is almost no limit to the design of this type of frame. To make a bamboo cane tower, simply push four canes of equal length into the plant pot and join the tops with a ring of wire keeping the canes vertical. For extra solidity, cut two pieces of cane and make a cross, the ends of which fit onto the tops of the four canes. Cones, pyramids, squares, and columns are easy. Use them as low-cost substitutes for traditional topiary frames, or fill in with chicken wire and cover them with climbers.

WIRE IS THE MOST VERSATILE MATERIAL FOR CONSTRUCTION. IT CAN BE

BENT INTO ALMOST ANY SHAPE DESIRED.

SMALL FRAMES COULD BE FASHIONED FROM

OLD COAT HANGERS, BUT

MAKING WIRE FRAMES

FOR LARGER PIECES,

IT'S BEST TO BEGIN WITH

PREVIOUSLY

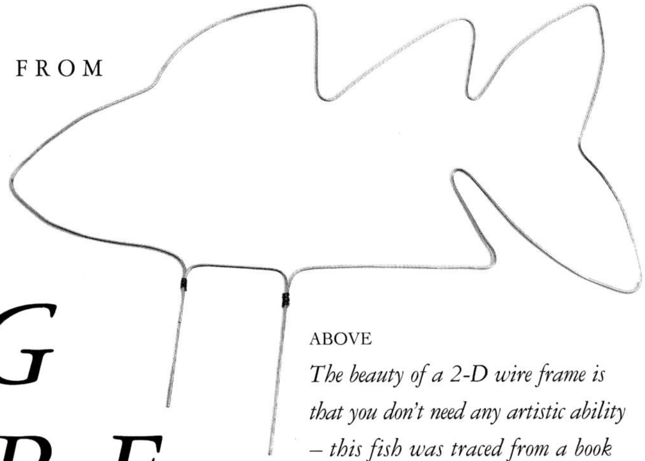

ABOVE
The beauty of a 2-D wire frame is that you don't need any artistic ability – this fish was traced from a book and enlarged using a photocopier.

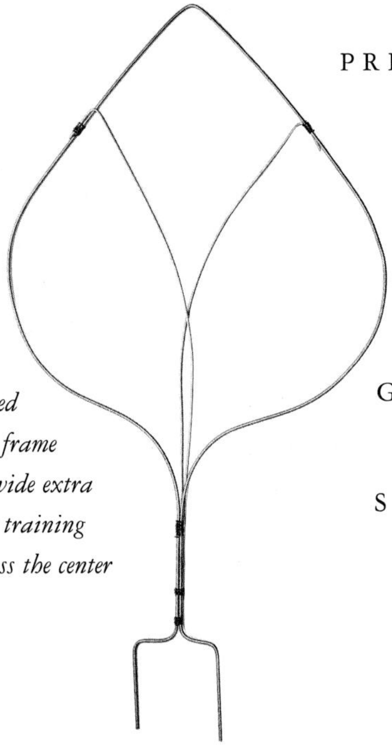

RIGHT
This botanical motif is very simple to make. The two stylized "veins" fixed within the frame outline provide extra support for training plants across the center portion.

UNBENT WIRE OF A GOOD LENGTH. YOU CAN BUY

THIS IN DIFFERENT GAUGES — THE HIGHER THE

GAUGE, THE THINNER THE WIRE. COPPER-COATED,

SOFT STEEL WIRE IS PARTICULARLY PLEASING.

LEFT TO RIGHT
Heavy duty wire
cutters; hammers;
stout, soft leaded
pencil or marker pen;
round-nosed pliers;
nails, preferably
headless; wire for
frame-making
(various gauges);
wire cutters; thin
spool wire for tying.

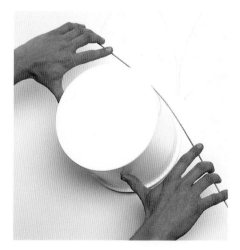

ABOVE
Smooth curves are achieved by bending the wire around ordinary objects like storage jars and paint pots.

There are no specialist tools required for frame-making on a small scale. In fact, much of what is needed can be found in an average household toolbox or garden shed. You may not need everything shown here, but a good pair of cutters and some round-nosed pliers will make all the difference, especially if you plan to make more than one or two frames.

Wire – for making the frames. This can be copper-coated, galvanized or plastic-coated. Wire is available in different gauges, or thicknesses. Gauge 10 or 12 was used for most of the frames shown.

Wire cutters – for cutting pieces of wire. Note that some "good" pruning shears also have a wire-cutting notch for thinner pieces. Some pliers too, have a useful cutting notch.

Round-nosed pliers – for shaping, gripping and twisting wire for topiary frames.

Spool wire – for tying off/together thicker pieces of wire in frame-making and also for "filling in" on wire frames to give extra support for plants.

Bamboo canes – for frame-making and support such as securely placing a wire frame into a hedge to make a finial.

Small-mesh chicken wire – for filling in hollow 2-D and 3-D shapes to give more solid-looking figures and provide extra plant support.

Pencil/marker pen and paper – for marking frame design templates.

Headless nails and a hammer – for making a former on which a frame design can be easily copied.

The heart is the ultimate symbol of romance,

love, and friendship. It is simple to draw

and so makes an ideal frame-making project with

which to begin.

EASY
HEART

Planted appropriately, it would make a

special gift for any number of occasions including, of course,

Saint Valentine's Day! These instructions

contain virtually all the techniques you need for making any

kind of wire frame.

Step one

Draw a heart onto paper to use as a template. Trace a piece of string around the outline, allowing extra length to the depth of your pot.

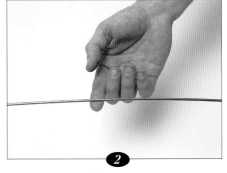

Step two

Cut your wire according to the length of the string. Find the center of the wire strand by balancing it across one finger.

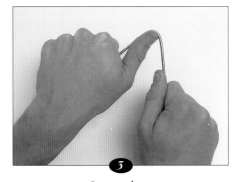

Step three

Bend the wire in the center by hand to form the "V" at the top of the heart.

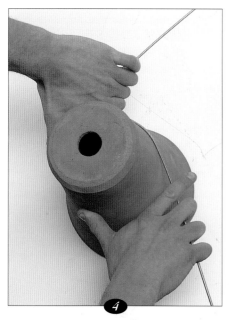

Step four

Using a plant pot or a similar round object, bend one half of the heart shape. You'll have to make the curve a little tighter than needed as the wire tends to spring back when released from the former.

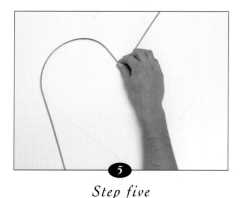

Step five

Place the frame against the template to check that it matches. Repeat steps 3 and 4 to make the other half of the frame.

Step six

Bend the two ends of the wire so that they meet. Then bend them so that they lie parallel to one another.

Step seven

Fasten the two ends together using spool wire. Leave a long end hanging down parallel to the stem of the heart frame and wrap the other end around all three strands several times.

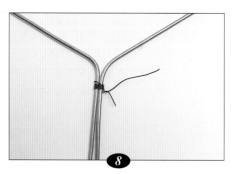

Step eight

Twist the two free ends of the spool wire around each other and trim off the excess with wire cutters. This is the standard technique used for securing all frame joints.

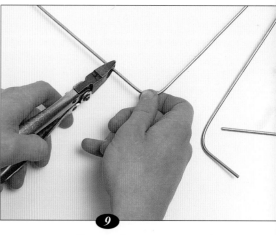

Step nine

Cut the ends of the heart frame to the required length. If it is to be used in a pot, it's a good idea to bend the ends outwards, to provide greater stability. Place the frame in the pot and then fill with potting mixture.

CHRISTMAS TREE

Planted in red or gold pots with deep green foliage, this little 3-D tree would make a wonderful tabletop decoration for Christmas. This design is easier than it looks. You don't even need a template because all you are doing is making a series of triangles, using the two free ends of wire as a guide.

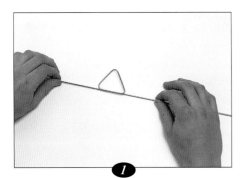

Step one

Make the first triangle (the top of the tree) and bend the free ends around so that they are parallel and overlapping.

Step two

Using round-nosed pliers, bend a series of gradually increasing steps down each side of the design. Make one step at a time, checking that the opposite side is a perfect mirror image by bending the two ends around so that they are overlapping and parallel.

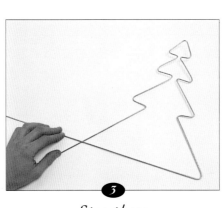

Step three

Continue until you have used up most of the wire, leaving just enough to set it in the pot.

Step four

Bend the free ends down to form the tree trunk and use a short piece of wire to bridge the gap. Secure in position with spool wire.

Step five

If you want to make several identical pieces, the process is much quicker and easier if you construct a frame around which the wire can be bent to the same pattern as the original. Keep in mind that you need room to maneuver the long piece of wire, so don't attempt to copy frames in which there is a dense concentration of tight bends.

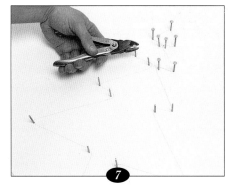

Step seven

Ideally, headless nails should be used, or otherwise, cut off the heads with a stout pair of wire cutters so that they don't get in the way. Be sure to wear safety goggles.

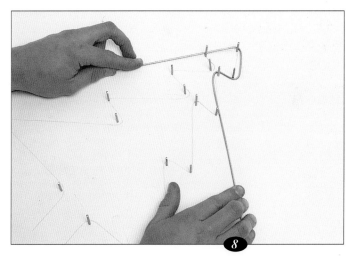

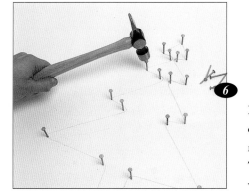

Step six

First trace the outline of the original frame directly onto a fiber board or similar material which can be hammered into. Then hammer in nails at all the points where the wire needs to be bent.

Step eight

Starting in the middle of the wire as usual, begin bending one half of the tree around the nails. Keep tension on the other end to stop the wire from slipping.

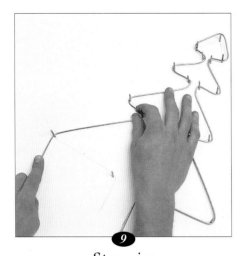

9

Step nine

Complete the other half and remove the copied frame from the former. You will probably need to flatten out the frame.

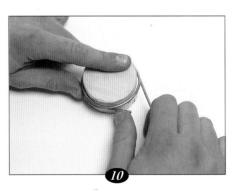

10

Step ten

Fashion a couple of wire rings to secure the middle and bottom of the frame. Use a round object to bend the rings to the required size.

Step eleven

The rings should overlap so that they don't show a gap when they expand slightly under their own tension.

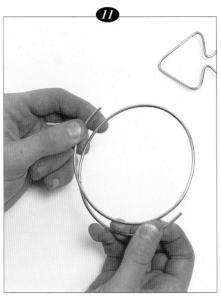

11

Step twelve

Tie the two frames together at the tip using tightly wound spool wire.

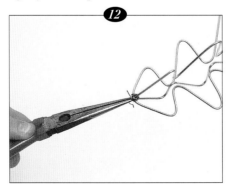

12

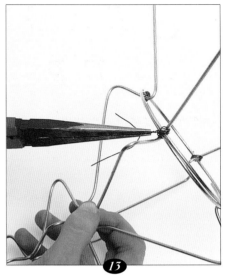

13

Step thirteen

Next fix the first of the wire rings around the frame to add stability. Tie it firmly in position with spool wire.

14

Step fourteen

Fix the second smaller ring in place around the neck of the frame and tie in as before.

HEAD FRAME

This unusual frame is sure to become a topic of conversation. Make even more of a statement by making two "talking" heads and setting them face to face. Cover with a small-leafed ivy or similarly delicate plant and leave the face uncovered so that the features are not obliterated. Alternatively, place over a small specimen of box or other traditional topiary plant, and clip it to shape as it grows.

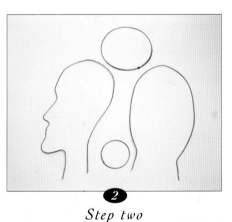

Step one

Bend a piece of wire around to form the back of the head, crown, and forehead. Then, using a pair of pliers, shape the profile.

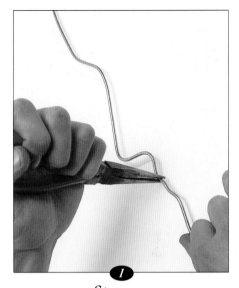

Step two

Shape another piece of wire to fit crosswise over the face frame, and then make two overlapping rings, one for the top of the head and one to fit around the neck. Join the frames together using spool wire in the same way as for the Christmas tree (opposite).

PLANTING FRAMES

The easiest and most versatile way of shaping greenery is to train it around wire frames. You can grow a very wide range of plants on frames, including hardy and tender shrubs, climbers and creeping ground-cover varieties.

LEFT

*Moss-filled frames can be planted with contrasting foliage to give a variety of textures. Here a spider plant (**Chlorophytum**) mimics the tail feathers of some exotic bird.*

RIGHT
*When planted, wire
frames produce a very
similar effect to
traditional clipped
topiary.*

Ready-made frames are available in a choice of

designs, most commonly geometric – cones,

spheres, pyramids, and so on – but also

stylized animals, birds, and even figures.

The basic techniques for using such frames

are demonstrated in the step-by-step

descriptions that follow.

TOOLS AND MATERIALS

Sphagnum moss – for filling topiary frames. This must be moist and green.

WHAT YOU WILL NEED OUT OF THE TOOLS AND

MATERIALS SHOWN BELOW IS REALLY DEPENDENT ON THE TYPE

OF TOPIARY YOU PLAN TO MAKE AND THE PLANTS BEING USED. FOR TRADITIONAL,

CLIPPED TOPIARY SHAPES USING WOODY PLANTS, YOU WILL CERTAINLY

Nylon fishing line – invisible and a good material for binding moss tightly within a topiary frame which has large gaps.

NEED PRUNING SHEARS AND

PROBABLY SOME KIND OF GARDEN

SHEARS. A PAIR OF SHARP SCISSORS

Bamboo canes – for attaching to the base of frames so that they can be firmly secured in pots or in the top of a hedge when training finials.

WILL NORMALLY SUFFICE FOR TRIMMING

SOFT SHOOTS.

Green plastic-coated twist ties – for easy attachment of stems to frame.

Pot fragments – for placing at the bottom of pots before planting to ensure good drainage.

Scissors – for removing or trimming back thin shoots during training, especially in framed and moss-filled topiary. For removal of dead foliage and flowers and for cutting pieces of twine for tying in.

Pruning shears – for shaping topiary, especially pieces too thick to cut with scissors, and trimming large-leafed plants like bay and holly which would be spoiled by shears.

Garden shears – for clipping. These should be small, "ladies" shears with pointed blades and need to be a dainty pair as they are easier for clipping fine detail.

Sprayer – for maintaining any kind of moss-filled topiary.

Horticultural aggregate – for hydroponic growth of plants to cover 3-D topiary frames and for filling gravel trays to create a humid atmosphere for moss-filled topiary.

Florist's wire – some should be cut and bent into "hairpins." Used for tying-in and for pinning shoots down onto the surface of moss-filled frames.

Soil – choose one suitable for containers and hanging baskets.

THE SIMPLEST FRAME DESIGNS ARE TWO-DIMENSIONAL
AND CONSTRUCTED IN SUCH A WAY THAT THEY FIT INTO PLANT
POTS OR DIRECTLY INTO THE GROUND.

PLANTING 2-D FRAMES

THE PLIABLE STEMS OF SHRUBS AND CLIMBERS ARE THEN TRAINED UP AROUND THE OUTLINE SHAPE. TO CONVERT AN OUTLINE INTO A SOLID FIGURE, THE SIMPLEST METHOD IS TO FILL THE SPACE BETWEEN THE UPRIGHTS WITH SMALL-MESH CHICKEN WIRE. PLANTS ARE THEN TRAINED ACROSS THE MESH UNTIL THE CENTER PORTION IS COMPLETELY COVERED.

RIGHT
What plant could be more appropriate for training over this romantic frame than **Abutilon megapotamicum** *'Variegatum?' The red and yellow heart-shaped flowers hang down like drop earrings amongst the prettily variegated leaves.*

LEFT
This copper butterfly appears to be flitting through the flowers lightly trained around its frame. **Plumbago auriculata***, the Cape leadwort, is a tender blue-flowered climber similar in appearance to jasmine. This is the white form 'Alba'.*

ABOVE
You needn't be too rigid about covering the frame outline precisely, especially when the foliage is as delicate as this jasmine.

2-D topiary can be very quick indeed to make. All you need is a trailing plant, a climber or lax-stemmed shrub with a quantity of long pliable shoots, and you can virtually cover a small frame immediately. You can either follow the design perfectly, tying the shoots in closely to the wire, or simply use the frame as a support and weave the stems loosely in and out.

2-D frames can be used in the garden, direct in the ground, or in pots. Indoors, try them in house plants as unusual ornamental supports for climbers and trailers.

ABOVE
Most house plants enjoy the steamy atmosphere of a bathroom, so why not pick a trailer or climber to cover a frame with a seashore flavor such as this fish. The creeping fig used here, with leaves reminiscent of overlapping fish scales, is ideal.

The jasmine covering this star-shaped frame is a hardy summer-flowering form, Jasminum x stephanense, which has attractively variegated new shoots and fragrant pink flowers.

A JASMINE STAR

If you wanted to use the frame for indoor decoration, then the highly scented Jasminum polyanthum, which begins to bloom just after Christmas, would be a good choice. Its many white blooms would create an effect like stardust on a magic wand. Jasmines are vigorous climbers, so you should not expect to maintain them on the same frame for more than a couple of years.

Step one

Cut the ties holding the jasmine plant to the cane supplied with the plant to support it and gently lay the long stems down, spreading them out evenly around the pot.

Step two

Cut off any short shoots at the base which cannot be tied into the frame.

Step three

Wind the stems around the upright of the frame and then secure them in place on the star using short lengths of florist's wire or plastic-coated twist ties.

Step four

Trim the foliage from the stems wound around the upright of the frame. Continue to wind in and trim shoots as they grow.

Step five

Continue until the whole of the frame head has a light covering of foliage. Tuck in any wayward shoots where possible. Otherwise, trim off any which stick out awkwardly. Don't be too rigid about this - jasmine foliage is delicate enough not to obscure the frame outline.

When covered with greenery, this easy-to-make frame looks very much like a slender poplar or cypress in outline. Two such frames, each planted in a small, square Versailles tub

AN IVY TREE

or classically-designed terracotta pot, would make a stylish pair of sentinels for either side of a doorway. The ivy used for this project is a particularly elegant form called Hedera helix 'Sagittifolia'.

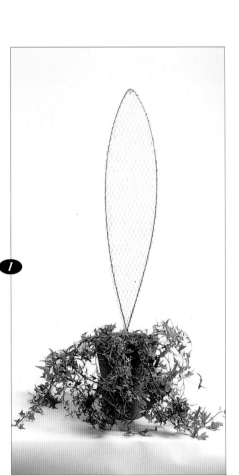

Step one

Cover an elliptical wire outline, like the one illustrated, with a piece of small mesh chicken wire as follows. Lay the mesh over the shape and cut around it leaving just enough overlap to turn the edges in over the wire. Wear thick gardening gloves as the cut ends are sharp. Splay the two ends of the frame out for extra stability.

Step three

Continue to tie in shoots as they grow until the whole frame is covered. The frame should be covered within a month or so.

Step four

From then on, trim the topiary occasionally to keep a neat outline. Stand in a position sheltered from wind to prevent the frame from being blown over.

Step two

Select a pot of trailing ivy. Those sold for hanging baskets, with many cascading shoots 3–3½ft (90–105cm) long, are ideal. Avoid plants trained up canes, as these tend to show bare sections of stem when untied. Push the ends of the frame into the root ball and cover the edges of the frame first. Then begin to cover the mesh, securing the ivy stems in place using plastic-coated wire twist ties or short lengths of florist's wire.

*Note~*The same technique for solid 2-D frames could be used to make other simple shapes, such as circles or domes.

PLANTING 3-D FRAMES

A VARIATION ON THE SIMPLE 2-D FRAME TYPE IS THE THREE-DIMENSIONAL FRAME WHICH IS AGAIN COVERED OVER WITH FOLIAGE GROWN FROM THE BASE, LEAVING THE CENTER HOLLOW. THESE FRAMES HAVE MORE IMPACT THAN THE 2-D TYPES AND THE SKELETAL FRAMEWORK HAS A SCULPTURAL QUALITY WHICH IS ATTRACTIVE EVEN WHEN UNCOVERED.

BELOW
If you stand a frame with a broad base on a bed of soaked hydroponic pebbles, you can cover it with ivy cuttings rooted directly in the pebbles and trained up over the frame.

ABOVE
Use moist sphagnum moss, wrapped tightly with nylon fishing twine to fill out narrow sections of frame and to give plants something to root into.

There are several ways to cover 3-D frames depending on the way they are constructed. The sitting dog opposite is covered in a close network of wires and can be treated like a solid figure, with plants attached to the outer surface using inconspicuous ties. If you grow cuttings in hydroponic pebbles as illustrated, spray with foliar feed to keep plants growing strongly.

Where there are larger gaps between the supports, you'll have room to wind the stems around. Ivy and other plants with stiff but flexible stems will stay in place on their own, but other types will need to be tied in. If these trained stems are pinched out, side shoots will develop and eventually fill in the spaces. Vines with tendrils or plants like the glory lily and clematis, which attach themselves by curling their leaf tips around supports, are perfect for frames with a more open network of struts.

Some 3-D frames have too few struts to train plants effectively, and you'll need to add in extra support. Do this with small-mesh chicken wire, fine spool wire, or nylon fishing twine.

LEFT
It's easy to cover wire frames with ivy. You don't need to tie the shoots in place, just wind stems around the supports.

RIGHT
The exotic glory lily **(Gloriosa rothschildiana)** *is a wonderful plant for training over large topiary frames. Specimens can be bought from florists and garden centers, but you'll need patience to untangle and detach the stems for retraining. It's much cheaper and easier to plant tubers in the spring and train the stems as they grow.*

COVERING A CHRISTMAS TREE FRAME

Ivy is an appropriate choice for this project since along with holly, it has strong associations with Christmas time. For instructions on how to make the frame yourself, see pages 20 to 22.

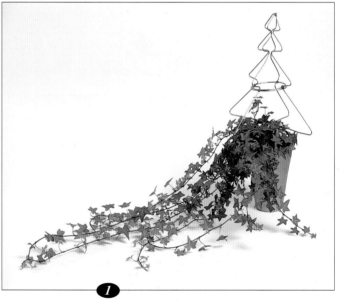

1

Step one

Choose a plant with plenty of long trails, well clothed in leaves. Spread the trails out, then insert the frame, pushing it firmly down into the soil.

Step four

It will take several days for the leaves to re-orientate themselves. Keep the topiary in a cool, well-lit position and spray frequently if the atmosphere indoors is dry.

Step two

Begin winding each trail around the individual wires of the frame. There's no need to tie the stems in place.

Step three

Continue the process, using several strands per wire until each is evenly covered in foliage. Try not to obscure the frame design. If you have spare ivy trails, cut them off and use them for propagation.

ROSEMARY GLOBE

Rosemary is a quick growing, wonderfully aromatic shrub, well suited to training. The young shoots are soft and pliable when young and can be molded to cover most geometric and 2-D frames. After about a year, the growth becomes woody, and the shape is fixed even if the frame is subsequently removed.

Step one

Select a young rosemary specimen that has plenty of unbranched shoots growing from the base - these will ensure even coverage. Try both the frame and plant in the pot to judge the correct planting depth. The base of the sphere should be just above the base of the plant.

Step two

When the plant is firmly in place, push the frame into the center of the root ball. Spread the stems out as evenly as possible around the frame. It won't be perfect, but any gaps can be covered over as new shoots grow.

Step three

Tie the shoots gently in place until the whole sphere is covered - green plastic-coated wire ties or pieces of soft green twine are ideal for this purpose.

Step four

You may need to provide extra support to fill large gaps in the frame. Use fine spoolwire or nylon fishing line, both of which will be virtually invisible when covered.

Step five

Place the rosemary globe in a sunny, sheltered position. If it's against a wall turn regularly to encourage even growth. Pinch out shoot tips to encourage side branches and continue to tie shoots onto the frame as they grow. When completely covered, maintain a neat spherical shape by pinching out overlong shoots with thumb and forefinger. Regular pinching out will help to prevent shoots from becoming bare and woody at the base.

Ivy was chosen to plant this egg-shaped frame, made from two hanging baskets, suitable for use outdoors, but you could also use all kinds of compact flowering bedding plants, such as Impatiens (Busy Lizzie), Begonia semperflorens or lobelia. The technique described below can be used to plant up all kinds of moss-filled topiary frames.

HANGING TOPIARY

Step one
Having removed the chains, place the basket in a pot for stability while you work. Line with a thick layer of sphagnum moss.

Step two
Next fill the center with multi-purpose potting soil and firm down well.

Step three
Take a pot of rooted ivy cuttings (this is how you generally buy ivy for bedding) and split the root ball to single out individual plants.

Step four

Take a stick or cane and make a hole through the moss into the potting soil to accommodate the ivy root.

IVY SPHERE

By joining two hemispherical hanging baskets together, you can make a perfect sphere-shaped frame for planting. It is such a simple idea, yet the result can look very attractive, especially when several identical spheres are hung in a row, along the line of a porch or pergola, for example. Ivy is one of the best subjects for moss-filled frames like this, as it roots readily from its stems and will still survive if the moss is occasionally allowed to dry out.

Step five

Push the cutting right into the hole. It helps if the neck of the plant is well covered by the moss. Continue this way until the whole basket is covered. Make another basket to match the first.

Step six

Join the baskets together with strong wire ties or self-locking electric wire ties.

Step seven

Reattach the original basket chains so that the topiary can be hung. Feed and water regularly to promote vigorous growth and trim to shape. Pinching out the tips will induce more bushy growth.

Note~To maintain even growth, remove chains and turn the sphere the other way around every now and then. Clip the ivy as required to keep a neat appearance.

TRAINING A CLIMBER OVER A MOSS-FILLED FRAME

This is an instant method for making small topiary features. Two or three of the little round-headed standards illustrated would make a delightful table decoration for a dinner party and would take no more than half an hour to make once all the components had been gathered together.

Step one

Plant a delicate-leafed climber such as this purple bell vine (*Rhodochiton atrosanguineus*) in an attractive pot. Another annual climber, the yellow-flowered, Black-eyed Susan (*Thunbergia alata*), would also make a good choice.

Step two

Soak fresh green sphagnum moss, then use it to fill the head of a sphere-shaped frame, packing it in tightly. You can hold the moss in position better if you bind the frame around with nylon fishing line which is virtually invisible.

Push the stem of the frame down firmly into the pot.

Step three

Wind individual trails around the stem and up over the head.

Step four

Secure the trails in position using pieces of florist's wire bent in half like hairpins. Simply push these into the moss.

ADAPTING TRADITIONAL TOPIARY

BELOW
The peacock is one of the classic topiary designs. These birds atop a yew hedge at Wardington Manor, Oxfordshire, in England would have taken several years to grow.

In this chapter, you'll be shown the easy way to create traditional topiary, on a scale appropriate for the garden and lifestyle of today. There are tips on how to speed up the process, interpret classic shapes, and detailed instructions for using a variety of frame designs and plants.

So if you want to create an obelisk of clipped greenery at the end of a path, a larger-than-life peacock in the middle of the lawn, or "finials" on top of a hedge, do not be afraid to try. Traditional topiary is usually of box or yew and ranges in design from large, intricate, sometimes fanciful, figures to the simple low hedges used to mark out the ground pattern in a classic herb garden or a parterre. If you're looking for inspiration, you can find plenty of fine examples in various historic gardens around the world. In the United States, the historic gardens of Williamsburg in Virginia are ranked highly. In Britain, two of the best-known examples of plant sculpting are to be found at Levens Hall in Cumbria and Hever Castle in Kent.

BELOW
On a smaller scale, you can make peacocks from box, using a simple traditional method (see pp. 48–49) or by planting up a ready-made wire frame.

QUICK RESULTS WITH BOX

When using a frame which is wider at the base than at the top, you can achieve quicker results by using several plants, rather than just a single specimen. For example, with a pyramid or obelisk, use four plants. After a while, the plants will merge together to form what looks like just one large plant.

1

Step one

Take three or more young box specimens – if you've grown your own plants from cuttings, you'll probably have some plants which are a bit lopsided. These "rejects" are ideally suited since their individual shape will be hidden on planting. Alternatively, start with smallish plants sold for hedging – these are relatively cheap.

Note ~ this technique can be used with other traditional topiary plants listed in the Plant Directory. *Lonicera nitida*, rosemary, forsythia and ligustrum will all form a cone shape in about five years or less. *Berberis thunbergii* and *Viburnum tinus* will also work well.

Step two

Plant as close together as possible in a container or direct in the ground. If you have a tall, thin plant, you could surround it with shorter, bushier specimens to construct a rough cone. Put the frame in place over the plants, pulling the longest shoots through the gaps working from the bottom to the top.

Step three

Feed and water regularly to speed up the production of new shoots. A cool, lightly shaded greenhouse will provide ideal conditions so long as the air is not too dry.

Step four

Trim back any shoots which have grown through the sides of the frame using pruning shears (do not remove leading shoots). This will encourage branching and the plants will thicken out.

Step five

Once the cone frame has been filled, maintain a neat outline by regular pinching out with thumb and forefinger, or trimming with a small pair of pruning shears. Frames that are wider at the base than at the top can be removed if desired.

Contrary to what you might think, it takes only a few simple steps to coax the

shape of a peacock from a bushy box or shrubby honeysuckle.

A   PEACOCK

Once the initial training has been completed, the figure will

become more defined as it grows and thickens out.

Step two

Bend a piece of heavy-gauge fencing wire to form the curve of the head and neck with a long straight piece to slot down inside the pot to secure it in place.

Step one

Choose an untrained or unclipped plant, preferably with a spreading rather than upright growth. Experiment by parting the branches down the middle. You should be able to see potential head and tail sections even at this stage.

Step three

Push the wire right down inside the pot on the side most suitable for making the front of the bird.

Step four

Next bunch together the stems at the back of the plant and fix a large wire hoop over them. Push the ends of the wire right down to the base of the pot.

Step five

Hold the branches in an angled fanned-out position by grasping both sides of the wire and bending the top half backwards. You will probably need someone to hold the pot steady while you do this as fencing wire is very difficult to bend.

Step six

Begin tying the branches to the S-shaped wire to form the head and neck. Take off any excess branches and trim to shape.

Step seven

Clip over the fan-tail section with pruning shears, removing shoots sticking out above or below the tail. Continue pinching out and clipping over the next few months so that the peacock shape fills out. Allow some shoots to grow from the top of the head to form the characteristic topknot.

MAKING A TOPIARY BASKET

The box-leafed holly, Ilex crenata, *makes an interesting substitute for more traditional topiary plants like yew, privet and box; some of the golden forms such as 'Golden Gem' demonstrated here are particularly attractive. Young plants tend to have an open, spreading growth, ideal for the purpose of training a basket shape. When properly filled out, like the fully grown ligustrum 'Jonan' (left), topiary baskets make original table decorations, perhaps for a dinner party, and could be filled with fresh cut flowers arranged in a moist block of florist's foam.*

Step one

Choose a young plant with an open center and at least one overlong shoot.

Step two

Fix a curved piece of heavy-duty fencing wire over the plant, pushing the ends right down to the base of the pot.

Step three

Next, attach a circle of wire around the plant, about a third to halfway up the hoop from the rim of the pot.

Step four

Leaving the long stem free to cover the basket handle, begin tying the remaining shoots to the circular wire. Space out the shoots growing from the base of the plant as evenly as possible to form the basket sides. Bend the upright stems down horizontally, left or right, and tie them onto the circular wire to form the rim of the basket.

Step five

Tie the long shoot over the wire hoop to begin covering the handle. You will need to keep tying this in as it grows.

Step six

Cut off any short shoots that cannot be tied into the frame to give a smooth outline. Also remove any crossing shoots in the basket base to produce a hollow center.

Step seven

Once all parts of the framework have been trained, all that remains to be done is to keep trimming back shoot tips which protrude from the basket surface. Feed and water regularly and keep in warm, light greenhouse conditions to promote rapid growth.

CLIPPING A CONE INTO A SPIRAL

Though more time-consuming than training plants over
forms, there are shortcuts that make it easier to create spiral-trained
specimens. In this case, early preparation of the plant selected for
training is essential. Otherwise, you may find when you cut into a
branch that you expose a hole that will take some time to fill out.

Some people will find it easier to clip simple shapes
by eye rather than using a guide as demonstrated here. If
this is the case, once you've made the initial shallow spiral
groove, you should find the rest of the clipping very easy.

Step three

Using a small, sharp pair of shears, begin clipping a broad spiral groove using the string as guide. Clip a little at a time so that you don't accidentally take off more than you want at each stage. Stand back from the plant occasionally to review your progress. When shaping a plant which is standing on the ground, it is easier to clip if the shears are turned upside down and to work from the tip to the base.

Step one

Take a bushy, well-shaped box plant approximately four years old from a cutting. Clip the plant into a cone shape and leave to grow on for a year, clipping with shears to maintain a neat, balanced outline.

Step two

Wind a piece of string around the cone, dividing it into three sections, gradually decreasing in depth towards the tip. You may need to repeat the process several times until the spiral looks right from all angles.

Step four

Remove the string and continue clipping, widening the groove and rounding off the edges. Trim the base of the plant right back to the central stem to give a short leg.

CONIFER CORKSCREW

This method of clipping a spiral results in an interesting effect: it seems as if a thick coil of greenery has been wound around a central wooden pole. The principle is the same as for the box spiral (see pages 52–53) with the difference that the groove is cut right in to reveal the central stem. Traditionally, yew is used as it has the necessary dense growth and ability to regrow from old wood. Speedier results can be obtained using relatively quick-growing conifers including Cupressus *and* x Cupressocyparis *cultivars.*

Step one

Begin with a young plant around three years old which still has the ability to regrow when pruned. We have used a young *Cupressus arizonica*.

Step two

Secure a long piece of ribbon or string to the pot and wind a spiral around the plant to act as a guideline for cutting.

Step three

Following the line of the ribbon, cut away all side branches as close to the main stem as possible using pruning shears.

Step four

Next cut off the tips of the remaining side shoots to encourage further branching and thickening out. The plant will look pretty threadbare at this stage, but if well tended through the first growing season, the corkscrew profile will gradually start to emerge.

Step five

Repeat this tip pruning once more during the growing season and also pinch off the ends of any side shoots which develop in response. Continue this pruning regime during subsequent growing seasons. In seven or eight years you will have a corkscrew like the large *Cupressus arizonica* in the main picture. Even the newly trained tree will look good in two or three years.

MAKING A STANDARD

STANDARDS ARE REALLY JUST A SPECIALIZED BRANCH OF TRADITIONAL TOPIARY. A SINGLE, WELL-GROWN STANDARD CAN MAKE AN IMMEDIATE IMPACT IN THE GARDEN, ADDING HEIGHT AND STRUCTURE TO A BORDER, FOR EXAMPLE. TWO MATCHING STANDARDS, THOUGHTFULLY POSITIONED, CAN TRANSFORM AN ENTRANCE.

RIGHT
*Golden privet (**Ligustrum ovalifolium** 'Aureum') – regular pinching out of the shoots at the top of the stem promotes bushiness and eventually a dense head develops.*

RIGHT
*The bright golden-green leafed **Cupressus** 'Goldcrest' can be clipped into an assortment of simple shapes. With the exception of yew, conifer training must begin with young specimens to ensure success.*

RIGHT
***Berberis thunbergii atropurpurea** with its attractive russet coloring, makes an unusual standard.*

RIGHT
*Make an even greater impression by training a double or triple ball standard like this gray-green leafed conifer, **Cupressus arizonica**. Ensure that the clipped spheres are large enough to balance the thickness of the stem. Otherwise, the topiary will look out of proportion.*

The simplest type of standard has a rounded or dome-shaped head and is grown from a hardy or tender shrub or tender perennial, commonly fuchsia, geranium or *Argyranthemum* (marguerite daisy). Tender perennials can make good-sized standards in only a couple of years, but full training of hardy shrubs tends to take much longer.

It's best to start off with a young plant (rooted cuttings are best for tender perennial plants like fuchsias) so that you can start training the stem up a cane keeping it perfectly straight from the beginning. You can also use larger, older plants provided they have a good strong upright stem growing up from the base. Just cut away the surrounding side shoots.

The aim is then to grow a single stem, known as the leader, to the desired height. Shortened side shoots and leaves developing along the length of the stem are sometimes left in position until the head has been formed, as this can help the stem to grow thicker and faster. Move into larger pots as the plant develops, and feed well. If you have a greenhouse or sun room, consider growing hardy plants under protection to accelerate their growth.

Depending on the size and vigor of the plant, the leader is trained up to 12in (30cm) beyond the final stem length. At this point, the growing tip is pinched out. This causes dormant buds below the tip to develop, and a mass of shoots grow out to form the head.

BELOW

Viburnum tinus is a superb shrub for training into a standard, with evergreen foliage and copious flower production during winter and spring. One of the advantages of training potentially large shrubs like this into standards is that they can be grown in a very restricted space.

RIGHT

The blue potato bush (Solanum rantonnetii) flowers from April to December and makes a pretty standard for pots in the sun room.

RIGHT

There is no reason why a standard head should be spherical in outline. Once the stem has been grown, you can shape the head in the same way as for traditional topiary. You can make it a spiral, cone, or pyramid, or combine different shapes, as this clipped atlas cedar (Cedrus atlantica) demonstrates.

RIGHT

This aromatic bay standard (Laurus nobilis) was made by training two shoots around a supporting stake to make a spiral. The same technique can be used for training climbers like Plumbago and honeysuckle into standards.

A FLOWERING STANDARD

The exotic-looking Brugmansia, *or Angel's Trumpet,*

makes an ideal subject for training into a standard. It is

extremely quick-growing and will reach the size of the plant in the main picture

in only two or three years. Take care when pruning this plant as all parts are

poisonous — wash your hands thoroughly after contact or wear gloves, and dispose of any

clippings safely. The enormous scented flowers can be appreciated all the more when

seen hanging down from the head below the level of the leaves. The same

principle applies to many other flowering plants, such as the commonly seen

fuchsias, or lilacs.

Step three

Remove any side shoots which appear along
the length of the stem as it grows. Cut back
as close as possible to the stem.

Step one

Choose a bushy, rooted cutting and select
one main stem for training, removing all
side shoots.

Step two

Insert a cane and begin tying in the stem as
it grows. Pinch out the growing point at the
end of the first season or beginning of the
next, once the stem has reached the desired
height.

Step four

The plant will flower in the second year
once the head has formed properly. The
flowering specimen shown was allowed to
produce a branch fairly low down the stem.
This gives the plant an interesting
asymmetric outline. For a more formal look,
all the side shoots would be removed.

Several different kinds of fruit can be trained as short standards and grown in pots in the greenhouse and on the patio, or as attractive and productive features in the flower garden or kitchen garden. As well as looking good, they can also be easier to maintain since spraying, pruning and cropping are all more accessible. Figs are ideal. They are very easy to grow, but untrained, tend to get far too big for most backyards.

A FRUIT
STANDARD

Many figs are very hardy, but you'll get a better quality of fruit if plants are grown in a greenhouse. Restricting the roots in a pot also restricts shoot and leaf growth, thereby encouraging fruiting and making it easier to manage plants. Embryonic fruits overwinter and mature the following year (late summer). Some people find the sap which exudes from cut fig leaves an irritant. If in doubt, use pruning shears and wash off any drips immediately.

Step one

Choose a fig from the garden center which has one good single shoot. Attach this to a cane to keep it straight. Don't allow any side shoots to form at this stage. Pot and feed well to encourage maximum growth of the leader.

Step two

Under good growth conditions, the plant may achieve the desired height in just one year. If it does, pinch out the top of the leader to encourage the formation of side shoots which will form the head. Otherwise, wait until next year.

Step three

Continue to remove any side shoots which form along the length of the stem.

Step four

Once the shoots forming the standard head grow five to six leaves, pinch out their tips. Once this pinching out has been done, the fig will begin to produce fruits. The fig shown here is just three years old.

CLIMBING
STANDARDS

A standard-trained grapevine makes a highly decorative plant

with its attractive foliage and hanging bunches of fruit.

Grapevines are very vigorous and if left unchecked quickly get

out of hand; conventionally trained vines require a great deal of space

too, so a standard is the answer in a restricted area. The shoots remain

within easy reach for pruning and the plants are

highly productive.

Step one

Start by buying a one-year-old vine from a garden center or nursery. Pot if necessary and ensure that the main shoot is properly supported by a sturdy support.

Step two

Pinch out all side shoots to one or two leaves from the main stem, but allow the leader to carry on growing. Tie in regularly.

Step four

Pinch out these side shoots and also remove any embryonic grape bunches that appear. In winter, about a month after leaf drop (between November and Christmas), cut back shoots forming the head to two buds from their origin. These then become the short "spurs" from which the shoots bearing the bunches of grapes develop.

Step five

In the third year, you can allow the vine to fruit, but restrict the number of bunches to one per shoot and only allow five or six shoots to develop. In order that these stems can support the weight of the fruit, support each one by tying the shoot tip to the top of the cane with soft twine. Alternatively, provide support with a frame designed for a weeping rose standard.

Step three

During the second year, continue to pinch out the side shoots as described in step 2. Once the main stem has reached the desired height, cut back the leading shoot. This encourages the production of many side shoots at the top of the plant which will form the standard head.

WISTERIA STANDARD
The wonderful specimen pictured here is only four or five years old, proving that you don't have to wait decades for the plant to flower. The trick is to start with a named, grafted cultivar of Wisteria floribunda *(this one is 'Alba').*

AN INSTANT MINI-LOLLIPOP

You can make instant standards simply by pruning

away the lower branches of a plant. The resultant

kinked and gnarled-looking stem

makes the plant look as though it's been

grown for many years, much like the effects

created by bonsai training methods. The plant

illustrated, Buxus sempervirens, *not the dwarf*

variety, is in fact only three years old

from a cutting.

Step one

Select a plant which has one good upright
stem. It doesn't matter if the base of the
plant has become pretty threadbare.

1

2

Step two

Remove stems growing from the base to expose the central main stem or "leg" of the standard.

Step three

Clip off any side shoots on the leg, leaving as short a stump as possible each time.

3

4

Step four

Next remove selected branches from the head. Proceed carefully at this stage and follow the branch you intend to cut, right through to the tip to make sure that it won't leave a big hole if removed. Turn the plant around as you work and try to imagine the final shape while you prune.

Step five

Continue until a more or less spherical head has been created. Don't worry about gaps; regular pinching out will fill in the holes to produce a dense head over the coming months. Remove any side shoots that appear on the leg using thumb and forefinger.

CARING FOR YOUR TOPIARY

BELOW
A pair of shears
make light work
of clipping fine-
leafed topiary
specimens such
as this box
cone.

Once you've created your green sculpture by whatever method, you will want to keep it in peak condition because by its very nature, it is bound to attract attention! With the guidance given in this chapter, many pieces can be maintained for years, but some types of green sculpture do have a relatively short life span. Planted moss-filled frames for example will need replanting from scratch every few years and ivy-covered sculptures eventually become too woody. The more frequently you check your topiary, the

more likely you are to spot potential problems before any real damage is done. However, apart from regular watering and feeding, some judicious pruning, and proper winter protection; relatively little maintenance is required.

ABOVE
This matching pair of box cones will need clipping several times a year to keep a sharp outline.

RIGHT
Raise outdoor pots off the ground to allow free drainage. Use small blocks of wood or terracotta "feet" like the ones illustrated.

POT-GROWN PLANTS

The main advantage of growing topiary in pots is mobility. You can move plants around to create different effects within the garden; bring outdoor topiary inside temporarily to decorate the house for special occasions; move tender plants to more sheltered positions during winter, and give house and greenhouse plants a vacation on the patio in summer. You can also take green sculptures off display while you carry out retraining or any maintenance work.

Growing plants in the relatively small soil volume of a pot does create a few problems though, the main ones being the need for frequent watering and feeding. Another is that in cold, exposed gardens, the root ball of a pot-grown plant is vulnerable to freezing, and if this condition is combined with wind, evergreen foliage can be damaged. Lastly, pot-grown plants will ultimately become too large for their containers and have to be potted on periodically if they are to remain in active growth.

CHOOSING A CONTAINER

Which design you choose is largely a matter of taste, but there are certain points to keep in mind when buying. Most importantly, a pot must have sufficient drainage holes to prevent waterlogging. It's also a good idea to raise containers off the ground slightly using small "feet;" otherwise the base can make a perfect seal with the ground, trapping excess water within the pot. Avoid containers with a narrow base as these can be unstable when planted with tall topiary, especially in windy gardens. Also steer clear of narrow-necked pots as the only way to get a pot-bound plant out again is by destroying the container!

Finally, when selecting a container, try to think about proportion and balance. What size and shape of pot would best suit the size and shape of your topiary specimen?

WHAT TO DO
WITH POT-BOUND PLANTS

To keep plants growing strongly, you'll need to continue moving topiary into larger pots as the roots fill the existing potting soil, a process known as potting on. Look for tell-tale signs such as roots growing out through drainage holes or plants which need very frequent watering and check by gently knocking the plant out of its pot. Select a container which is no more than two sizes larger than the existing pot and plant as described above taking care not to disturb the root ball. If you want to keep a fully grown topiary piece in the same container, simply top-dress every spring with fresh potting soil. Remove from the pot and carefully scrape away any loose soil,

ABOVE
To check if a plant needs to be potted on, gently knock it out of its pot and examine the roots. This specimen is clearly pot-bound.

ABOVE

To avoid rapid moisture loss through the walls of terracotta pots, line the sides with thin plastic sheeting.

being careful not to damage the roots, and repot with fresh soil.

WATERING AND FEEDING

Whether plants are growing indoors or out, it's a good idea to get into some sort of daily maintenance routine so that pots are not accidentally overlooked. Erratic watering is very damaging to plants in containers and potentially lethal. Outdoors, during hot summer days, small pots may need watering up to twice a day. Even on cooler, gray days, plants can dry out quickly, especially if it's windy and it's a mistake to expect rainfall to provide sufficient water. Mulching with a layer of bark chippings or gravel can help to retain moisture, but makes it more difficult to tell at a glance if the plant needs a drink. Terracotta pots dry out more quickly than other kinds, so to prevent moisture escaping through the porous walls, line pots with plastic before planting.

With so much water washing through

pots in summer, the soil rapidly becomes nutrient depleted. For quick, healthy growth, topiary plants need a steady supply of plant food – either use a slow-release chemical fertilizer with trace elements, applied once in spring, or a liquid feed, given regularly through the growing season. Topiary grown in the ground should also be fed at the start of the season unless the soil is very rich or regularly manured. Again a slow-release chemical feed or for organic gardeners, a dressing of fish, blood and bone fertilizer, should be applied.

Follow manufacturers' instructions and avoid overfeeding, as the resultant soft, sappy growth is more vulnerable to pest and wind damage. Nitrogen-rich feeds, in liquid or granular form, produce rapid growth for foliage varieties, but you'll need to choose a more balanced feed for flowering types. Otherwise, you may end up with lots of shoot growth and no blooms. Finish feeding

ABOVE

Applied at the start of the growing season, slow-release fertilizer spikes or pellets will feed potted plants right through to fall.

LEFT

Fine spray moss-filled topiary daily to keep the moss and plants fresh and green.

hardy, outdoor plants by the end of August so that tender new growth has sufficient time to toughen up before the winter.

WATERING MOSS-FILLED
TOPIARY FRAMES

Frames with plants inserted directly into the moss and potting soil filling are the most difficult to keep moist. Like hanging baskets, they need regular watering and liquid feeding to keep the plants growing strongly. In the early stages, when the frame is only partly covered, it's also important to keep the moss moist and green. The best way to water both plants and moss is to stand the topiary with its base in water to allow the moss and potting soil to soak it

up. Between waterings, spray the moss and plants at least once a day. To reduce the risk of directly planted, moss-filled frames drying out, stand the topiary on containers of moist gravel or porous horticultural aggregate (glazed ceramic dishes designed for bonsai work are ideal). For free-hanging topiary, position out of strong sunlight and wind and ensure that it can be easily taken down for soaking.

PINCHING OUT, CLIPPING AND TRAINING

The precise details of training for the various kinds of topiary are dealt with in the relevant chapters, but some ongoing pruning and training is necessary to keep plants in shape. With standards and traditional topiary, it isn't always necessary to maintain the shape by clipping with shears, especially with small pieces. Pinching out the tips of shoots which start to grow out of line is also a very effective method. Use your thumbnail or a pair of scissors or pruning shears. Regular pinching or light clipping is

the best way to keep traditional topiary and the heads of standards bushy and dense. Larger traditional topiary may need to be clipped two or three times a year if you want to maintain a very crisp, formal outline.

The type of plants chosen for moss-filled frames usually grow very close to the surface, following the contours, but will need the occasional haircut with sharp scissors. Pin down any wayward shoots using lengths of florist's wire bent in half. Check plastic-coated and wire ties regularly, especially on quick-growing subjects such as fuchsia standards where a stem can expand so quickly that the wire cuts in and strangles the plant.

CLIPPING LARGE-LEAFED PLANTS

Larger-leaved plants such as holly (*Ilex*), sweet bay (*Laurus nobilis*) and Portugal laurel (*Prunus lusitanica*) can be trained formally to make large topiary pieces, but only for simple shapes as the foliage is too coarse for detailed work. Clipping with garden shears is not ideal as this leaves unsightly cut edges. Use pruning shears to trim back individual shoots.

OVERWINTERING TENDER PLANTS

In a sun room or greenhouse, reduce watering and keep air somewhat more dry from fall through winter, otherwise plants may succumb to fungal diseases and start to rot.

If you don't have a heated greenhouse or sun room, tender topiary must be kept in the house during winter. Deciduous specimens such as figs and *Brugmansia* (syn *Datura*) may be stood out of the way in an unheated bedroom while dormant. As the foliage starts to drop, reduce the watering to a bare minimum and resume in spring once new growth appears. Some evergreen topiary plants may need more warmth (see Plant Directory for minimum temperatures), but can suffer in heated rooms because of low light levels, dry air and fluctuating temperatures caused by radiator heating. Warmth encourages growth, but because of the lack of light, new shoots tend to be pale and drawn. Move indoor topiary as close to a window as possible, but protect shade-lovers from strong, direct light and keep all topiary away from radiators or cold drafts. In heated rooms, maintain humidity by standing topiary pots on a gravel tray and by spraying. Do not feed as this will encourage premature growth.

OVERWINTERING HARDY PLANTS

Even technically hardy plants can be damaged by winter weather, and unless you live in a very mild, sheltered spot, it's best to take some precautions. In exposed gardens, move pot-grown specimens against a warm wall, or better still, into an unheated greenhouse. Protect stems of standards by putting foam pipe insulation on them or by wrapping with layers of horticultural fleece. Evergreen topiary planted in the ground may be protected from wind scorch by erecting windbreak netting on three sides or by making a wigwam of canes around the plant and covering it with layers of horticultural fleece or hessian.

FIRST AID

Even with the best of care, topiary is still likely to need the occasional spot of first aid to keep it looking in tiptop condition. In late spring, check planting for winter damage – pick off dead or scorched leaves

LEFT
To prevent frost damage, wrap pots in a thick layer of insulation such as several sheets of styrofoam or plastic garbage pail bags stuffed with straw or crumpled newspaper.

and prune back any dead shoots, but don't be too hasty as some apparently dead stems on evergreen plants can resprout later on. Check by scraping back a tiny piece of outer bark. If the shoot is alive, the exposed section will be bright green. Delay clipping new spring growth damaged by frost until all risk of frost has passed. Otherwise, the shoots which regrow may be hit again, weakening the plant further.

EMERGENCY MEASURES

If a whole section of plant dies out in a moss-filled topiary frame, either remove all the dead material and replant that section, or train shoots from surrounding plants to fill in the gaps. If you want the topiary to be on show for a party, say, but the damage is still visible, camouflage the bald area by pushing pieces of cut plant material (soaked for several hours beforehand) into the moist moss. Hold in place using florist's wire pins. The plants should remain fresh-looking for at least a day, more if regularly sprayed. Similarly, with ivy-covered frames which aren't quite full enough but which are needed for display, you can cheat by winding cut trails around to cover the bare patches. Remove once the cut material starts to flag visibly.

FILLING GAPS PERMANENTLY

Sometimes stems die back leaving unsightly holes in traditional clipped topiary pieces and the heads of standards. If this happens, cut away the dead portion and carefully bring some of the surrounding shoots across to fill the gap.

Topiary frames come in a wide choice of designs and a wide variety of materials. At the top of the range are ornate Victorian-style frames treated to look like antiques – you could happily leave these unplanted and use them as unusual garden sculptures. Then there are more simple frames, 2-D and 3-D designs made from galvanized or plastic-coated wire that resist rusting. You also occasionally see frames made from bamboo canes, wicker, plastic, or wood.

A DIRECTORY OF SHAPES

ABOVE
If you don't have the time to train a flowering standard, why not use a ready-made frame such as this and plant it with summer bedding?

American topiarists have the widest selection of frame designs and can choose from mail order lists which include traditional wirework figures like the peacock or rabbit to more outlandish creations such as dinosaurs, cross-legged elephants, and alligators standing on their hind legs! (See list of suppliers, p.124, for names and addresses of frame manufacturers.)

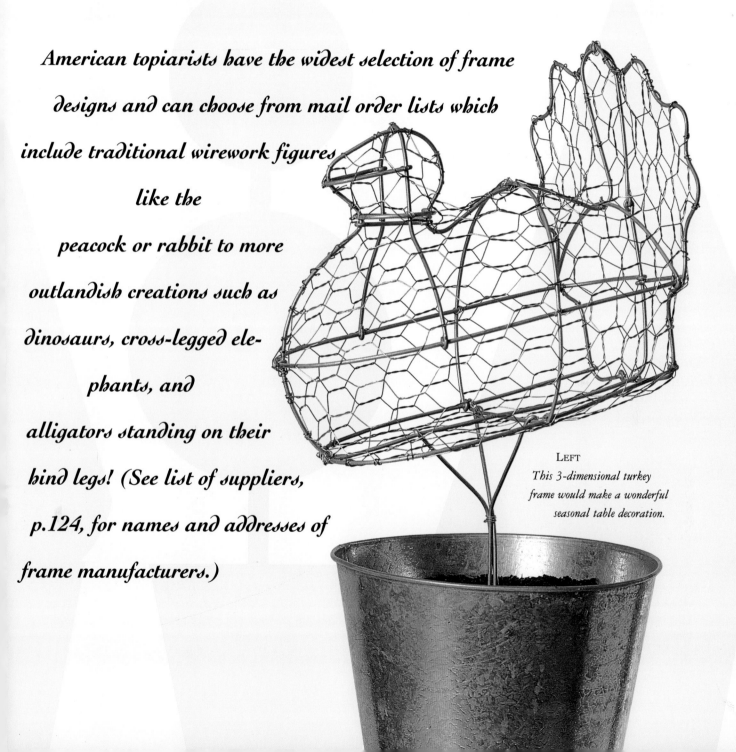

LEFT
This 3-dimensional turkey frame would make a wonderful seasonal table decoration.

THE CLEAN LINES OF GEOMETRIC SHAPES MAKE THEM SOME OF THE MOST DRAMATIC AND EFFECTIVE OF ANY TOPIARY DESIGNS. THEY ARE THE CLASSIC GREEN SCULPTURES, FITTING INTO ALMOST ANY STYLE OF GARDEN, FROM ROMANTIC AND ITALIANATE TO ULTRAMODERN.

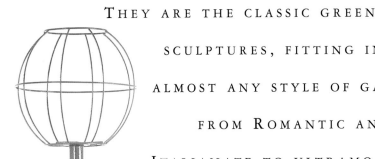

LEFT
Quick to make, these potted ivy globes add a touch of formality to the garden, especially when spaced at regular intervals.

RIGHT
This large, spherical-headed frame comes ready-lined and is ideal for adding height to containers on the patio or for training climbers.

GEOMETRIC

IN THE BORDER, GEOMETRIC TOPIARY DESIGNS WORK BEST WHEN KEPT FAIRLY TIGHTLY TRAINED OR CLIPPED SO THAT THE CONTRAST BETWEEN SURROUND FOLIAGE AND FLOWERS IS VERY MARKED. GROWN IN POTS, LARGER PIECES LOOK STRIKING AGAINST MASONRY AND WHEN USED IN PAIRS TO HIGHLIGHT FEATURES SUCH AS DOORWAYS AND ARCHES OR A GARDEN SEAT.

You can buy a wide range of ready-made topiary frames in geometric designs - globes, round-headed standards, double and triple balls, cones, spirals, and obelisks. These range from plain and simple structures to highly ornate pieces which you would be loathe to cover completely! Such frames can be used for training climbers, trailers, and so on, or as a guide to clipping. When clipping simple shapes like globes and cones, you don't always need a frame. Some shrubs naturally produce a rounded, dome-shaped, or conical outline, and you may already have such plants in the garden which with a little clipping or pruning can be coaxed into a perfectly regular geometric form.

To create a series of small globes, for example, as path edging, try cotton lavender (*Santolina chamaecyparissus*), *Berberis thunbergii* 'Atropurpurea Nana,' or *Euonymus fortunei* 'Emerald Gaiety.' For clipping easy cones, pick shrubs like common box, Portugal laurel (*Prunus lusitanica*), holly, and bay.

ABOVE
It only took a few minutes to train this pot of trailing ivy over the cone-shaped frame.

LEFT
A variation on the cone – this reproduction of an original Victorian frame would be particularly suited to a period garden.

BELOW
One of the best ways to grow climbers in pots on the patio is to train them around simple topiary frames. This scented evergreen climber, **Trachelospermum jasminoides**, *takes on a much more attractive form when trained around a spiral frame.*

ABOVE
A mini ivy standard in the making – the beauty of wire frames like these is that even in the early stages, the skeletal framework gives a strong idea of what the finished piece will look like.

RIGHT
*It's a mistake to cover some frames completely, as the intricacy of the design can be lost among the foliage. This delicate looking twirled and twisted frame is lightly draped with the appropriately named "hearts on a string" (**Ceropegia woodii**).*

ABOVE

Geometric shapes likes these box globes contrast strongly with the softer lines of the surrounding planting. Equally spaced on either side of the path, they make the whole design stronger by emphasizing the symmetrical layout and will add interest in winter when the herbaceous plants have died down.

ANIMALS AND BIRDS

ANIMALS AND BIRDS HAVE ALWAYS BEEN POPULAR SUBJECTS FOR GARDEN ORNAMENTS AND SCULPTURES, BUT THERE IS SOMETHING ESPECIALLY APPEALING ABOUT "LIVING" CREATURES. GIVING AN ANIMAL TOPIARY PIECE AN APPROPRIATE POSITION IN THE GARDEN ADDS GREATLY TO ITS EFFECTIVENESS. FROGS AND TURTLES LOOK WELL NEXT TO WATER, AND CATS COULD BE HALF HIDDEN AMONG THE FLOWERS OR CATNIP.

LEFT
You could cover the body of this larger than life wicker bird with a delicate ivy, leaving the large fan tail as a contrast.

LEFT
This pair of hounds leaping over the border plants are expertly fashioned from single box plants. If you have difficulty training by eye, use a ready-made topiary frame for guidance.

The texture and color of an animal sculpture are also worth careful consideration. A scaly reptilian skin could be mimicked using succulents like the knobbly gray-leafed *Sedum spathulifolium* 'Cape Blanco' in a moss-filled frame, and a small, furry or woolly animal could be created by planting a frame with a froth of tiny leaves such as *Soleirolia*. Long fur or a bushy tail can be represented with fine-leafed grasses like the blue-gray *Festuca glauca* and spines by tussock-forming sedges such as *Carex oshimensis* 'Evergold.' A contrast in texture can also be achieved by clipping to different degrees over the body in the same way that a toy poodle is clipped.

Whatever plants you choose, the important thing to remember is not to let the foliage become so luxuriant or unkempt that the outline of the animal is lost, so a sheep, for instance, really will need shearing! And, if you plan to display your animal topiary among other plants, it's best to go for a plain or dark-leafed plant that will contrast well. Variegation can confuse the eye, just like camouflage patterns on a

ABOVE
This bird outline frame is very simple but at the same time very striking. It needs to be given a plain backdrop in the garden to show it to the best effect.

RIGHT
This giant rabbit is made from a moss-filled frame planted with variegated **Euonymus fortunei** *'Emerald Gaiety' which, like ivy, has stems which root where they touch.*

BELOW
*By planting different sections of moss-filled frames with contrasting plants or by leaving some sections bare, you can define the shape more clearly. This little turtle frame is a perfect example – only the "shell" has been planted, in this case using a plant which is just right for the job – the bead plant (**Nertera grandensis**).*

RIGHT
*Even if you don't have a garden, topiary can be created using houseplants like this variegated Mind-Your-Own-Business (**Soleirolia soleirolii**) whose mossy growth is ideal for covering smaller frame shapes.*

soldier's uniform.

Similarly plump bird shapes have always appealed to the topiarist, even if the exact species is not always identifiable! The most simple designs are nesting ducks, geese, owls, and chickens. These solid shapes are ideal for moss-filled and planted topiary as there are no long narrow sections to cause problems with drying out. For long-necked birds such as herons or swans, or birds with outstretched wings, it's best either to train in the traditional manner or to cover the frame with small-leafed climbers grown up from the base. The fine details of frames such as heads with top-knots and beaks, are sometimes better left uncovered. Otherwise, they can become obscured by foliage. In the garden, ducks, geese, and swans can be made to look as though they are swimming by setting them on a flat "pool" of low-growing ground-cover plants.

The fan-tailed peacock is one of the classic topiary figures. You can buy ready-made wire frames in a peacock design for traditional topiary or for covering with climbers. Alternatively, see pp. 48–49 for step-by-step instructions on how to train a peacock using bent wire.

The texture of feathers is relatively easy to mimic, provided the leaves are relatively small and closely overlapping. The Snakeskin plant, *Fittonia*, is perfect for small moss-filled topiary because its net-veined leaves look very similar to feathers. Flecked and mottle-leafed ivies also give a similar effect.

RIGHT

For a whimsical touch, you could plant a whole group of rabbit frames and plant them in the vegetable patch among the lettuce and carrots!

RIGHT

Animal topiary figures set around the garden will delight children, and if they want to have a try too, frames like this simple squirrel outline would make an easy project for them to start with.

LEFT

In order to show the detail, small moss-filled animal frames are best covered with fine-leafed plants such as the variegated Mind-Your-Own-Business (**Soleirolia soleirolii** 'Variegata').

LEFT

Because the gaps between the wires are very small, this galvanized wire dog frame is best covered by filling with moss and training plants like creeping fig or ivy over the outside.

LEFT

It's very important not to obliterate the fine detail of an animal frame. Otherwise, it can become unrecognizable. Here only the body has been planted and there's just a little ivy trained over the wing outline. If you want to, you can camouflage the struts of a wire frame by binding it with clumps of moist moss.

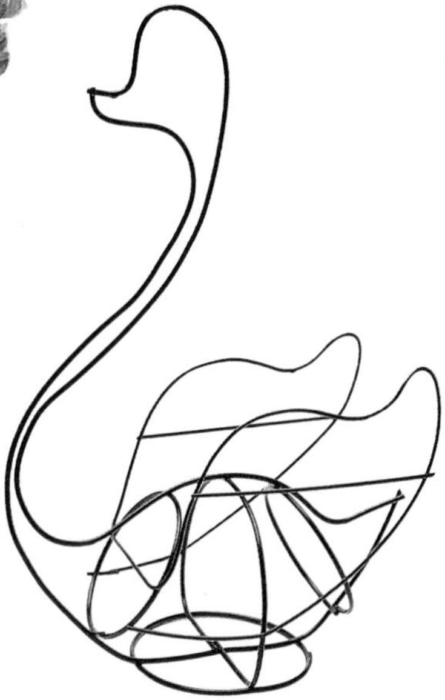

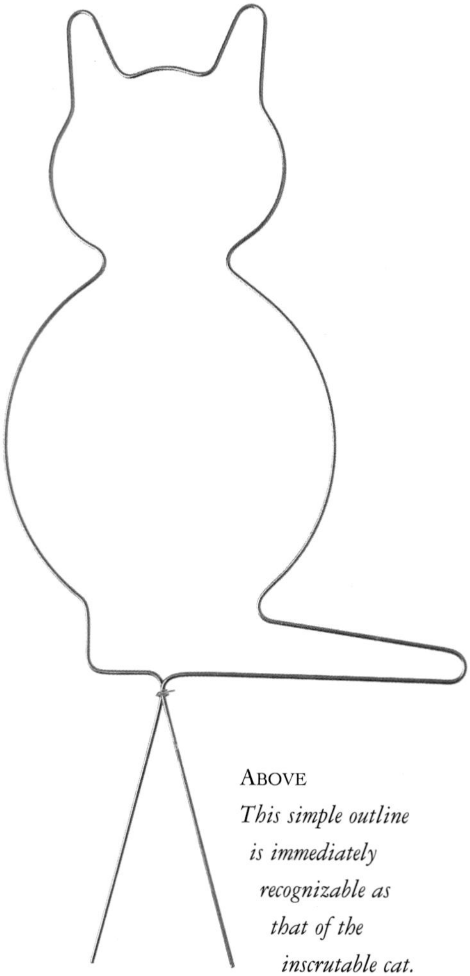

ABOVE

This simple outline is immediately recognizable as that of the inscrutable cat. For fun, why not position it in front of a fake mouse hole painted onto a wall or fence?

LEFT

This topiary frame has been used as a guide for training a young box plant. The supple stems have simply been fed through to the inside of the frame, and any wayward shoots have been trimmed off.

THERE ARE TOPIARY DESIGNS WHICH CAN BE ADAPTED TO VIRTUALLY ANY OCCASION, SO WHY NOT SURPRISE FRIENDS AND FAMILY BY GIVING A CUSTOM MADE GREEN SCULPTURE INSTEAD OF CUT FLOWERS OR MORE CONVENTIONAL GIFTS? MAKE IT EXTRA SPECIAL BY DECORATING THE POT OR ATTACHING RIBBONS TO A FREE-STANDING PIECE.

SPECIAL OCCASIONS

YOU CAN GET VIRTUALLY INSTANT EFFECTS WITH QUICK-TO-CONSTRUCT COVERED WIRE FRAMES OR MOSS-FILLED FRAMES, BUT IF YOU'RE MAKING TOPIARY FOR A SPECIFIC DATE, ENSURE YOU ALLOW SUFFICIENT TIME FOR THE PIECE TO FILL OUT AND FOR THE LEAVES TO REORIENTATE THEMSELVES. A HEART IS ONE OF THE EASIEST FRAME SHAPES TO CONSTRUCT — PERFECT FOR SAINT VALENTINE'S DAY!

LEFT
*The prettily variegated Snakeskin plant (**Fittonia albivenis** 'Nana') is an ideal subject for covering moss filled frames.*

LEFT
This 3-D heart is a slightly more complicated version of the 2-D frame shown step-by-step on pp. 18–19, but is still easy to construct.

Two hearts intertwined would not be much more difficult and could be planted to celebrate an important wedding anniversary, for example. Similarly for Christmas, you could take a traditional motif such as a star and plant it with gold-variegated ivy or make small moss-filled cones covered in dark green foliage.

Either would look stylish as table decorations for Christmas day – try spray-painting plastic pots in gold or festive red and decorate the miniature Christmas trees with tiny baubles.

There are lots more ideas in the step-by-step sequences that follow.

If you are stuck for ideas as to what to make for someone's birthday, for example, and can't find a ready-made frame that suits you, think about that person's interests and try to come up with a relevant shape on which to base your design. For example, they could be very fond of animals, they may collect something for a hobby, or have a passion like music, gardening, travel, or sport. Once you've settled on your motif, create a template on paper, keeping it as simple as possible. Use books and magazines for inspiration. An even easier alternative would be to make a frame of the first letter of their name.

BELOW
As an exciting and unusual alternative to a traditional Christmas tree, why not dress up your topiary with lights and decorations?

Like the Christmas tree frame, this free-standing angel would make a delightful table decoration. Spray the frame gold or silver beforehand and leave the wings and halo uncovered. Fill the body with moss and potting soil and plant cuttings directly through the sides.

LEFT
With a small frame like this, it wouldn't take long to train a plant such as box up through the middle to create an authentic looking Christmas tree.

ABOVE
This Christmas tree frame with its red candles and covering of variegated ivy would make a wonderful table centerpiece for the festive season. The plastic pot and sprigs of ivy at the base have been spray-painted gold for extra sparkle.

ABOVE

Hung on a door, this wreath would make a delightful welcome to a summer garden party or barbeque. The trailing nature of **Lysimachia nummularia** makes it an ideal subject.

ABOVE

Teddy bears appeal to all ages, but planted, this character could be the center of attention at a children's party. Add a couple of eyes pushed through the frame with wire and dress him up for the occasion with a big bright bow tie.

RIGHT

This cuddly teddy bear made from ivy could be used to decorate the house or garden. Initially, you'll need to train the stems over to cover any bare patches, but once covered, all you need to do is to clip off or pin down any wayward shoots.

THE PLANT DIRECTORY

RIGHT

*A standard fall flowering chrysanthemum (**Dendranthema**) about to burst into bloom. These and their close relatives, the marguerites (**Argyranthemum**), make showy, long-flowering standards.*

The list of plants in the Directory is by no means exhaustive, but it gives a good selection of the wide range of subjects that can be used for quick and easy topiary.

LEFT
Three different varieties of Mind-Your-Own-Business
(Soleirolia soleirolii, S.s. 'Variegata,' and S.s.
'Aurea') make an intriguing pattern across the
surface of this circular planted topiary.

Your choice of

plant is governed

by the type of green

sculpture you wish to

create and here are a few

guidelines for choosing the

appropriate plant (the

different training

methods are dealt

with in detail in the relevant

chapters).

HOW TO USE THE DIRECTORY

THE PLANTS IN THE DIRECTORY ARE LISTED ALPHABETICALLY BY THEIR LATIN NAMES. ALL OF THE INFORMATION YOU NEED ABOUT THE PLANT IS CONTAINED UNDER THE HEADINGS DESCRIBED OPPOSITE. THE FLEXIBLE NATURE OF TOPIARY MEANS THAT YOU DO NOT HAVE TO BE RESTRICTED BY YOUR LOCAL CLIMATE TO THE USUAL RANGE OF PLANTS THAT YOU CAN GROW IN THE OPEN GARDEN. YOU CAN CHOOSE FROM MANY MORE TENDER PLANTS THAT CAN BE CONTAINERIZED AND BROUGHT INDOORS OR INTO THE GREENHOUSE OVER THE WINTER.

Botanical name is international and the form given is the one usually used in nurseries and garden centers. **Common name** (in parentheses) is the name used by most people to refer to the plant. **Minimum winter temperature** and the hardiness zone are given after the symbols. It is important to remember that these are only a guide. A plant's ability to survive certain temperatures is also affected by factors like protection from wind and the amount of insulation given in winter. **Uses** shows what type of topiary the plant is suitable for. Some plants, such as ivy, are versatile enough to be used for any purpose. **Characteristics**

describes the general growth, foliage, and flowers of the plant, plus recommended alternative varieties. At the end of the section is an indication of the height and spread which plants can be expected to attain in a reasonable time period (10 years maximum for woody subjects, about a year for ground-cover plants). **Training** gives specific training and pruning information. **Cultivation** gives details of any specific requirements and notes on propagation.

Symbols at the top of each plant entry give the following information at a quick glance:

 Evergreen (retains leaves throughout the winter)

 Deciduous (loses all leaves in winter)

 Semi-evergreen (loses leaves in very severe weather)

 Flowering period if applicable (numbers denote months)

Patio (tender plants that can be placed outside in summer)

Full sun Requires full sun

Light shade Tolerates light shade

Moderate shade Tolerates light to moderate shade

Three quarter shade Tolerates deep shade

Full shade Tolerates full shade

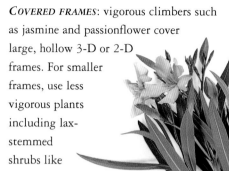

COVERED FRAMES: vigorous climbers such as jasmine and passionflower cover large, hollow 3-D or 2-D frames. For smaller frames, use less vigorous plants including lax-stemmed shrubs like rosemary.

MOSS-FILLED FRAMES: if you're covering the outside, you can use the same kinds of plant as for covered frames, but those with adventitious roots (produced from the stem) will eventually grow into the moss and produce a neater, more compact outline. To plant directly into the frame, pick a plant which spreads close to soil level and preferably roots as it grows, such as ivy or fittonia.

TRADITIONAL TOPIARY: requires a shrub with a dense, twiggy growth covered in relatively small leaves with the ability to reshoot from old wood when pruned.

STANDARDS: vigorous woody-stemmed shrubs such as forsythia and *Hydrangea paniculata* make excellent flowering standards while evergreens such as bay and holly provide year-round interest. Fruiting plants like grape or fig make standards that are both decorative and productive. The most appropriate height of the stem or leg is given, but many shrubs can also be trained on shorter stems for quicker results.

ABUTILON HYBRIDS
(Flowering maple)

Minimum temperature **20°F/–5°C** Zone **9**

Uses Flowering standards.

Characteristics Large plants for the greenhouse which are best grown in pots moved out to the patio during summer. Bell-shaped, white, red, orange, yellow, pink or purple flowers. The mid-dark green or yellow- (occasionally white-) variegated leaves are lobed or maple-like. Summer is the main flowering period, but there are intermittent flowers throughout winter. Varieties include 'Ashford Red' (red), 'Boule de Neige' (white), 'Canary Bird' (yellow), 'Nabob' (plum purple) and *Abutilon pictum* 'Thompsonii' (orange flowers with yellow-marbled leaves). 2–4ft (60–120cm) stem

Training Hard prune the standard head in late winter.

Cultivation Grow in potting soil. Propagate by taking 3–4in (7.5–10cm) cuttings of semi-ripe side shoots.

ABUTILON MEGAPOTAMICUM
(Trailing abutilon)

Minimum temperature **32°F/0°C** Zone **10**

Uses Flowering standards, covered frames.

Characteristics Tender shrub with twiggy, cascading branches, delicate green foliage and pendulous red and yellow, bicolored, bell-shaped flowers. Normally trained against a warm wall in Zone 10. It can also be grown as a pot or greenhouse plant and summered outdoors, or as a standard or over a frame.
3–4ft (90–120cm) stem when grown in pots

Training The plant will need permanent support for its main stem. Thin out head to maintain balance and an attractive shape and tidy up any winter damage during spring.

Cultivation Grow in potting soil. In the North, bring pots indoors before frost and overwinter in a frost-free place. Propagate by 3–4in (7.5–10cm) cuttings of semi-ripe shoots in summer.

AJUGA REPTANS
(Bugleweed)

Minimum temperature **–40°C/–40°C**
Zone **3**

Uses Moss-filled frames.

Characteristics Prostrate ground-cover plant forming rosettes of rounded green, purple-bronze or variegated leaves and runners that root where they touch the ground. Plants are deciduous in the North, evergreen in the South. The short, upright flower spikes normally in shades of blue appear between spring and early summer and are attractive, but may need to be removed to maintain the outline of the topiary. Purple-leaved varieties are available, such as 'Atropurpurea.' Prettily variegated, but less vigorous forms include 'Variegata' – buff, gray-green and cream, becoming pink-tinged in winter (the best variegated Ajuga for shade) and 'Burgundy Glow' – reddish-pink, pale pink and cream. 5–6in (12–15cm) when in flower × 18–36in (45–90cm), depending on variety.

Training Pinch off flower buds as they form.

Cut away any dead foliage in spring when new growth has resumed. Pin down runners to cover frame.

Cultivation Grow in a soil-less and potting soil mix with some hanging basket potting soil added. Keep moist at all times – the plant will not tolerate dry shade. Propagate either by division or by potting up rooted runners.

ARGYRANTHEMUM
(*Marguerite daisy*)

Minimum temperature **32°F/0°C** Zone **10**

Uses Flowering standards.

Characteristics Formerly listed under Chrysanthemum, these bushy, woody-stemmed plants have single, double or anemone-centered (raised central disc) daisy flowers in white, pink or yellow. Some of the newer, more unusual shades in peach and red are not as suitable for standards as they have a poor growth pattern. The green to gray-green or silver-blue foliage is divided, and in some varieties reduced to very fine thread-like leaflets. Some dwarf-growing kinds could be used to make mini-standards.

One of the best varieties for standards is *Argyranthemum frutescens* (white, single flowers). Another excellent choice is the vigorous sugar-pink 'Vancouver' with anemone-centered flowers and green foliage. 2–4ft (60–120cm) × 2–3ft (60–90cm)

Training Pinch out shoot tips to encourage formation of a bushy dense head once stem of

standard has been trained to desired height.

Cultivation Grow in potting soil. Pink-flowered types like 'Vancouver' as well as peach and red shades will fade unless given semi-shade. Propagate by 4in (10cm) softwood cuttings taken in early fall; pot singly when rooted. Use these cuttings to create standards.

AZALEA
(deciduous Rhododendron cultivars)

Minimum temperature **–10°F/–24°C** Zone **6**

Uses Flowering standards.

Characteristics Highly decorative shrubs with green foliage producing large trusses of bell-shaped flowers in shades of yellow, orange, red, pink and white. For scent, grow *Rhododendron luteum* which has yellow flowers and good fall foliage. For a wide range of colors, try the Knap Hill and Exbury cultivars or Mollis hybrids. 2–3ft (30–60cm) stems

Training Remove dead flowers and trim off any over-vigorous shoots.

Cultivation Grow in acid potting soil. Never allow the plants to dry out; spray with a mist of water during hot, dry periods. Propagate by semi-ripe cuttings taken in midsummer.

BERBERIS THUNBERGII VARIETIES

Minimum temperature **–20°F/–21°C** Zone **4**

Uses Standards, traditional topiary.

Characteristics Bushy, dense shrubs with small, rounded leaves in green, gold ('Aurea') or purple (*B.t. atropurpurea*). Variegated forms include 'Rose Glow' with purple, pink and cream mottled leaves. The dwarf purple-leafed 'Atropurpurea Nana' grows to 18 × 24in (45 × 60cm) and is suitable for making mini-lollipop standards. A profusion of small, pink-tinged white flowers with red calyces appears in early to mid-spring, sometimes followed by glossy red fruits. 8 × 8ft (2.5 × 2.5m) after ten years; gold and variegated leaf varieties are slower growing.

Training Clip to desired shape or train as standards, pruning the head, removing the occasional three- to four-year-old stem in spring to encourage new, bushy growth.

Cultivation Grow in potting soil and avoid very dry conditions. Propagate by semi-ripe cuttings in summer.

BRUGMANSIA
(Angel's trumpets)

Minimum temperature **20** to **15°F/ –7** to **10°C** Zone **10**

Uses Flowering standards.

Characteristics Quick-growing shrubs best grown in tubs or large pots. They produce large, pendulous, flared blooms in white, pink, apricot, orange or yellow and substantial green foliage. Many forms highly fragrant, especially at night. All parts of the plant are poisonous.

Recommended are: *B. sanguinea* – yellow, deepening to bright orange-red at tips, unscented; *B. suaveolens* – large single white, fragrant; *B. versicolor* (now *B. arborea*) – clear pink flowers and long yellow buds, fragrant. 4ft (120cm) stem

Training Once the plant has been trained to about a 4ft (120cm) stem, pinch out tip to encourage formation of head. Thereafter, prune branches of head back hard in spring (pollard) to keep in shape.

Cultivation Grow in any good fertile potting soil. Do not overfeed as this discourages flowering. Water freely during the growing season, very sparingly in winter, especially if plants have dropped their leaves. Where they are not hardy, move them to a greenhouse in fall or let them overwinter without leaves in a cool room indoors. Propagate by 4–6in (10–15cm) cuttings of young, semi-ripe shoots in late spring and root in a heated propagator.

BUXUS
(Boxwood)

Minimum temperature **–10°F/–24°C** Zone **6**

Uses Traditional topiary, standards.

Characteristics Classic evergreen topiary plant with fine, dense foliage ideal for producing topiary of good detail. As well as the common green box *(Buxus sempervirens)* and dwarf box, *B. sempervirens* 'Suffruticosa,' there are a number of other varieties which can be used for shaping. *B.s.* 'Rotundifolia' is slightly quicker growing with larger leaves giving a coarser appearance. 'Elegantissima' has creamy-white variegated foliage.

Training Use small, sharp garden shears or sheep shears to trim plants to shape in summer.

Cultivation Grow in well-drained potting soil mix. Variegated plants do best in light shade. Propagate by 3–4in (7.5–10cm) cuttings taken in late summer, which can be rooted in a shady cold frame or in a sheltered, shady corner directly in the ground.

CEANOTHUS
(Californian lilac)

Minimum temperature **–10°F/–24°C** Zone **7**

Uses Flowering standards.

Characteristics Group of vigorous, deciduous or evergreen shrubs, varying in degree of hardiness and flowering time. Choose hardier evergreens with small glossy leaves and fluffy blue flowers between late spring and fall. Good deciduous varieties include *C.* x *delileanus* 'Gloire de Versailles.' Will easily make standards with 4–5ft (120–150cm) stems

Training Remove winter-damaged stems from evergreens in spring. Cut back side shoots after flowering to control shape and size of standard head. With deciduous plants, cut head back hard in spring to a framework of branches.

Cultivation Grow in potting soil. Protect plants grown in pots under glass in winter. Propagate by semi-ripe cuttings taken in summer.

CERASTIUM TOMENTOSUM
(Snow-in-summer)

Minimum temperature **–50°F/–46°C** Zone **2**

Uses Moss-filled frames.

Characteristics Vigorous carpeting alpine with a profusion of white star-like flowers during late spring and summer. Small silvery-gray leaves.
3–4in (7.5–10cm) high, spread indefinite.

Training Cut back any over-vigorous growth and pin stems into position.

Cultivation Grow in potting soil and propagate by division in the spring.

CESTRUM
(Jessamine)

Minimum temperature **22°F/– 5°C** Zone **9**

Uses Flowering standards.

Characteristics Deciduous or evergreen shrubs and scramblers, often trained against a south- or west-facing wall or grown in pots. Long drooping clusters of tubular flowers that are scented in some varieties; colors are pink, purple, red, orange, or greenish-yellow. Good varieties are:
C. elegans (syn. *C. purpureum*) – light purple-red flowers followed by red berries;
C. 'Newellii' – bright carmine-pink flowers;
C. parqui – deciduous shrub with greenish-yellow, night-scented flowers good for a conservatory. *C. parqui* 3–4ft (90–120cm) tall, others potentially much larger but easily pruned and shaped into weeping standards 4–5ft (120–150cm) tall.

Training Thin out standard head in early spring by removing a proportion of two- or three-year-old stems. At the same time, trim back all side branches to 6in (15cm).

Cultivation Grow in well-drained potting soil. Provide a sunny, sheltered site in summer. Propagate by cuttings of semi-ripe side shoots. 3–4in (7.5–10cm) long in July–August. Root in a heated propagator.

CLIANTHUS PUNICEUS
(Lobster Claw, Parrot's Bill)

Minimum temperature **40°F/4°C**   Zone **10**

Uses Flowering standards.

Characteristics Climbing shrub with handsome, evergreen foliage divided into many small leaflets. Clusters of scarlet-red claw-like flowers early summer. Forms with colored flowers such as the white ('Albus') are also available.

4 ft (120cm) stem

Training Trim or thin as necessary in summer to keep plants to required size.

Cultivation Grow in well-drained potting soil. Water freely in summer, but keep plants drier in winter. Spray foliage to lessen likelihood of red spider mite attack and keep greenhouse-grown plants well ventilated during warm weather. Propagate from seed in early spring – they will flower in two to three years' time. Alternatively, take 3in (7.5cm) long semi-ripe heel cuttings using side shoots and root in a heated propagator in summer.

COPROSMA × KIRKII 'VARIEGATA'

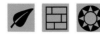

Minimum temperature **37–41°F/2–5°C**
Zone **10**

Uses Standards.

Characteristics Low, spreading/weeping shrub with dense, pretty, green and white variegated foliage. If male and female plants are grown together, mistletoe-like berries form in fall.

3–4ft (90–120cm) stem

Training Pinch out shoot tips to encourage bushy standard head.

Cultivation Grow in well-drained potting soil. Propagate by semi-ripe heel cuttings in late summer.

CORREA

Minimum temperature **38–40°F/3–5°C**
Zone **10**

Uses Flowering standards.

Characteristics Australian shrubs with small green leaves and hanging, tubular, pink, white or greenish flowers. Some types have felted stems and leaf undersides. Good varieties are: *C. alba* (Botany Bay Tea Tree) – white flowers, the form 'Pinkie' has white flowers flushed pink; *C. backhouseana* – long yellow-green blooms, hardier than most; *C.* 'Mannii' – reddish-pink bells; *C. pulchella* – pink flowers.

3–5ft (90–150cm) stems

Training Pinch out shoot tips to promote bushy standard head.

Cultivation Grow in neutral to acid, well-drained potting soil. Water sparingly when plants are not in flower and avoid overwatering at other times. Use rainwater if in hard water area. Will flower year-round if under glass. Propagate by seed in spring or semi-ripe cuttings in summer.

deciduous

semi-evergreen

evergreen

flowering
period
months

patio

COTONEASTER CONSPICUUS 'DECORUS'

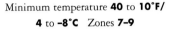

Minimum temperature **–10°F/–24°C** Zone **6**

Uses Traditional topiary, standards.

Characteristics Spreading, evergreen shrub with arching, much branched stems covered in small, deep green, glossy leaves. A profusion of tiny white flowers appears in late spring followed by many long-lasting red berries. *C. microphyllus* has similar foliage and naturally forms a low-spreading hummock. It can be trained into a weeping standard on 2½ft (75cm) stems or used for simple topiary shapes.

1–4ft (30–120cm) × 8ft (240cm)

Training Prune freehand to desired shape, or use a simple 3-D frame as a guide.

Cultivation Grow in well-drained potting soil and avoid waterlogged soil. Propagate from semi-ripe cuttings during summer.

CUPRESSUS
(Cypress)

Minimum temperature **40** to **10°F/ 4** to **–8°C** Zones **7–9**

Uses Traditional topiary, standards.

Characteristics Upright-growing conifers with dense, feathery foliage in varying shades of green through to gold. Varieties suitable for topiary include the yellow-green *C. macrocarpa* 'Goldcrest' and the gray-green *C. arizonica* var. *arizonica* and forms. Other quick-growing conifers that could be tried for topiary include × *Cupressocyparis leylandii,* the gold Leyland cypress, 'Castlewellan' and other forms, plus varieties of Thuja.

6–8ft (1.8–2.5m) tall

Training Train young specimens only into spirals and standards. Old, established plants in the garden are unlikely to regrow and cover bare areas.

Cultivation Grow in potting soil and keep container-grown plants well watered, but avoid waterlogging. The minimum temperature tolerated depends on variety. Propagate in the fall and spring with cuttings taken from the current year's growth.

CYTISUS
(Broom)

Minimum temperature **0°F/−18°C** Zone **7**

Uses Flowering standards.

Characteristics Flowering shrubs with fine, arching or upright evergreen stems and small, narrow green leaflets in threes. A profusion of pea-like flowers appears during late spring to early summer. Colors can be white, yellow, red, brown, orange, pink and mauve, and blooms are often bicolored. Good varieties include the vigorous forms of *Cytisus* x *praecox* such as 'Allgold' (yellow). 3–4ft (90–120cm) stems

Training Maintain shape of standard head by light pruning after flowering. Do not cut into old wood, pruning within 2–3in (5–7.5cm) of previous year's growth.

Cultivation Prefers deep, rich, well-drained soils; avoid highly alkaline soils. Propagate by softwood cuttings in early summer.

ELAEAGNUS

Minimum temperature **0°F/−18°C** Zone **7**

Uses Standards.

Characteristics Evergreen or deciduous shrubs, usually strongly upright-growing covered in dense, silvery-green or variegated foliage. The tiny, inconspicuous white or yellow flowers are highly fragrant and produced in fall. Plants may be damaged by cold winds so avoid exposed positions. Good evergreen varieties include the plain, gray-green *E.* x *ebbingei* and its variegated forms including 'Gilt Edge.' *E. pungens* 'Maculata' is also variegated. 4–6ft (120–180cm) stem

Training Remove winter damage in spring and shape using pruning shears.

Cultivation Grow in potting soil and avoid extremely alkaline soils. Some variegated varieties are less hardy and require some winter protection. Propagate by semi-ripe cuttings in spring and early summer.

EUCALYPTUS GUNNII
(Gum tree)

Minimum temperature **10°F/−12°C** Zone **8**

Uses Standards.

Characteristics Fast-growing tree with light gray-green, aromatic foliage. Normally stooled (cut back hard) to promote production of a mass of stems with rounded, juvenile-type foliage. Left to grow naturally, makes a slender tree with sickle-shaped adult foliage. Small young plants with no sign of being pot-bound are best. 3–4ft (90–120cm) stem

Training Once stem and head have formed, cut back the stems hard to form the head each spring. Pinch out over-vigorous shoots early summer.

Cultivation Grow in rich, moisture-retentive potting soil. Do not let pot-grown plants dry out during summer. Propagate by seed.

KEY

full sun

light shade

moderate shade

three quarter shade

full shade

KEY

deciduous

semi-evergreen

evergreen

**flowering
period
months**

patio

EUONYMUS FORTUNEI

Minimum temperature **–20°F/– 29°C**
Zone **5**

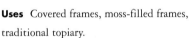

Uses Covered frames, moss-filled frames, traditional topiary.

Characteristics Low-growing evergreen shrubs usually grown as ground cover, but which may climb if grown against an upright surface. Best varieties include the yellow and green variegated 'Emerald 'n' Gold' and the more shade-tolerant green and white variegated 'Emerald Gaiety' (both pink-tinged in winter). In severe winters plants may lose a proportion of their leaves. 2 × 6ft (30 × 60cm) when grown as ground cover

Training Clip to shape in spring. Pin down shoots to cover stuffed frames, or for hollow, 3-D and 2-D frames, tie in shoots to frame as they grow. Remove winter-damaged shoots in spring.

Cultivation Grow in potting soil and avoid very dry conditions. Propagate by softwood cuttings.

FICUS CARICA
(Fig)

Minimum temperature **0°F/–18°C** Zone **7**

Uses Fruiting standards.

Characteristics Woody shrubs grown for their sculptural, deep green foliage and succulent fruits which ripen in fall. Many varieties exist, but very few are widely available. Of these, 'Brown Turkey' is amongst the most hardy and reliable with brown-skinned, pear-shaped fruit. 'Marseillaise' has large, almost spherical, fruit, pale green to yellow-white when ready to eat. There are several other fig varieties well worth seeking out with more ornamental fruit. Plants left outdoors in winter in the northern part of their range need protection.

3–6ft (90–180cm) stem

Training Remove surplus shoots in summer and cut back young fruit-bearing shoots to between four and five leaves in early summer.

Cultivation Grow in potting soil. Water and feed pot plants generously through the growing season. Hardiness varies, but even tender varieties can be overwintered successfully in a frost-free garage (no light is required as plants are not in leaf). Propagate by layers from mature plants grown in the ground, or from heel, semi-ripe cuttings 4–6in (10–15cm) long, taken in early fall and rooted in the cold frame.

FICUS PUMILA
(Creeping fig)

Minimum temperature **40°F/5°C** Zone **10**

Uses Moss-filled frames.

Characteristics Small-leaved trailer or self-clinging climber with deep green foliage that roots where it touches the ground. An ideal candidate for covering frames stuffed with moss and potting soil. Keep out of direct sunlight to avoid scorching and spray frequently. *Ficus pumila* 'Variegata' has bright, white-edged leaves. Will revert to plain-leaved form if grown in deep shade. At least 2 × 2ft (60 × 60cm) and much more under ideal conditions

Training Pin new shoots to the surface of the frame as they grow and pinch out shoot tips to encourage branching.

Cultivation Grow in potting soil mix that is kept moist at all times; spray frequently. Propagate by 2–4in (5–10cm) long cuttings from side shoots in late spring and root in a pot covered with a plastic bag in a warm room or in a heated propagator.

FITTONIA ALBIVENIS 'NANA'
(Snakeskin plant, Nerve plant)

Minimum temperature **60°F/15°C** Zone **10**

Uses Moss-filled frames.

Characteristics Creeping plant with small, green, white-veined leaves. This variety is much more tolerant of dry air conditions than its larger-leafed parent. Remove flower spikes: they detract from the foliage effect. 1 × 6in (2.5 × 15cm) or more

Training Pin down shoots to cover topiary frame. Cut off any stray shoots.

Cultivation Grow in a moisture-retentive potting soil mix. Keep mix moist at all times, but not wet, and avoid overwatering in the winter. Spray frequently and stand topiary on a tray of moist pebbles. Keep plants out of direct sunlight, which will scorch leaves. Shoots root where they touch the soil surface. Propagate by detaching rooted segments or take cuttings and root in a heated propagator in spring.

FORSYTHIA X INTERMEDIA

Minimum temperature **–20°F/– 28°C** Zone **5**

Uses Flowering standards.

Characteristics Common spring-flowering shrubs with mid-green foliage and bright yellow flowers in profusion. Good varieties for training into standards include 'Lynwood' and 'Spectabilis.' 4–5ft (120–150cm) stem

Training Immediately after flowering, cut back head to within 2–3in (5–7.5cm) of the previous year's growth.

Cultivation Grow in potting soil. Propagate by hardwood cuttings in fall and winter or softwood cuttings in summer.

FUCHSIAS

FUCHSIAS ARE PROLIFIC FLOWERERS AND WITH THEIR DANGLING BLOOMS LIKE SO MANY TWIRLING BALLERINAS, THEY MAKE SUPERB STANDARDS FOR THE SUMMER GARDEN.

LEFT
F. 'White Pixie' - a charming variety with dangling white bells topped with light cerise-pink sepals.

BELOW
F. 'Alice Hoffman' - popular hardy variety, dwarf, compact and floriferous with rose pink sepal and a "skirt" of semi-double white petals.

RIGHT
F. 'Grandma Sinton' - a lovely old-fashioned looking fuchsia with marshmallow pink semi-double petals, lighter colored sepals and contrasting deep pink stamens.

LEFT
F. 'Winston Churchill' - the sumptuous, fully double flowers have a "skirt"-like deep purple satin overlaid with cerise-pink sepals.

Almost any bush or cascade variety can be trained into a standard – the stem length is determined by the vigor of that particular variety and by the amount of growing time given before the shoot tip is pinched out to form the head. Stake the stem firmly from the beginning of training.

IGHT
'Lye's
nique' - a
ry old, vigor-
s variety, with
profusion of
ngle flowers
ith a long
be and stiff,
xy sepals in
hite and con-
sting deep pink
als.

RIGHT
F. 'Thalia' - a tropical-looking triphylla-type fuchsia with long, tubular flowers in large clusters and bronzy foliage. Will stand a sunny situation.

FUCHSIA

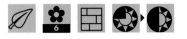

Minimum temperature **39–45°F/4–7°C**
Zone **10**

Uses Flowering standards.

Characteristics Plants frequently used in containers outdoors in summer bedding displays especially where summers remain cool and moist and overwintered as soft shoot cuttings or trimmed-back stock plants. Foliage is plain green, variegated, or bright lime green and flowers are drooping, composed of two distinct portions – an outer ring of four reflexed sepals and an inner tube of petals. Protruding stamens give the flowers an exotic appearance – there is a variety of colors: white, pink, red, orange, and purple; flowers are often bicolored.

Plants are woody and will form round-headed or weeping standards of varying sizes if the stem is given adequate support. Such plants will continue to flower in a sun room right through winter if a high enough temperature is maintained. Feed regularly throughout the flowering period using a high potassium (potash) liquid fertilizer. For details of Fuchsia varieties, see pages 102-103.

Training Train as a standard by the usual method, but to grow a stout stem, leave a number of shortened side shoots along its length until established. Prune head to shape in early spring. Weeping standards may be trained using a framework of wires.

Cultivation Grow in potting soil to give standard plants in pots stability. Keep soil moist but not waterlogged during the flowering season to avoid bud drop. At the end of the season, gradually withhold water and cease altogether when plants have lost their leaves. Resume watering in spring. Alternatively, if high enough temperatures can be maintained (55°F minimum), keep plants growing through the winter, but take care to avoid overwatering; a cool room in the house will do if you don't have a greenhouse. Maintain a humid, but well-ventilated atmosphere for plants grown in a sun room or greenhouse during the summer. Propagate by softwood tip cuttings, preferably without flowers, at virtually any time of year. Root in multi-purpose soil in pots covered with a plastic bag on a warm windowsill.

HEDERA HELIX VARIETIES
(Ivy)

Minimum temperature **0** to **10°F/
–18°** to **–24°C**   Zone **6-9**

Uses Covered frames; moss-filled frames, standards.

Characteristics Climbers/trailers with small, lobed green or white-, cream- or gold-variegated leaves. The stems root wherever they touch the ground. See pages 106-107 for a list of the best varieties for topiary. 4 × 3ft (120 × 90cm) and often much more

Training Wind shoots around frame or pin into position to cover moss.

Cultivation Grow in potting soil; for stuffed frame topiary hanging basket potting mixture can be used. Keep plants well watered during the growing season, but avoid over-watering especially in winter. Spray frequently to deter red spider mite and encourage rooting in stuffed frame topiary. Hardiness depends on variety: plain green-leaved types are hardier than variegated forms. Propagate by rooted runners or softwood cuttings taken in late summer.

HELIOTROPIUM ARBORESCENS
(Heliotrope, Cherry pie)

Minimum temperature **45–50°F/7–10°C**

Zone **10**

Uses Flowering standards.

Characteristics Tender shrubs generally grown as annuals. Handsome, deeply veined, glossy dark green leaves and clusters of small fragrant flowers in a variety of colors including shades of pink and purple, and white.

2–3ft (60–90cm) standards, with 12–15in (30–37.5cm) wide heads

Training Using rooted cuttings, stake the stem and remove all side shoots as it grows to the desired height. Then pinch out the tip of the plant 3–4 leaves above top of stem. When the side branches grow out, pinch out the tips again at the 4–5 leaf stage.

Cultivation Grow in potting soil. Plants under glass in summer dislike hot conditions. Propagate by 3–4in (7.5–10cm) long cuttings in fall or late winter and root in a heated propagator.

HOYA CARNOSA
(Wax plant)

Minimum temperature **45–50°F/7–10°C**

Zone **10**

Uses Covered frames.

Characteristics Climber with thick, waxy green leaves on twining stems that eventually adhere to walls by aerial roots. Stems are leafless at first and should not be removed. Intriguing pinky-white blooms with crimson-red centers like plastic flowers hang in clusters and produce copious nectar. Do not cut dead flowers, more flowers may be produced from the same site. *H. carnosa* 'Variegata' with creamy-white edged leaves is less vigorous than the species and does not flower as freely. Flowers produced intermittently from spring to fall. Grows to 15–20ft (4.5–6cm) so suitable for training on large frames.

Training Pinch out shoot tips of young plants to promote branching. Be careful about what surface you leave the plant on after training, as broken stems and leaves "bleed" sap. Gently wind the sinuous stems around the

frame as they grow.

Cultivation Grow in potting soil mixed with peat and perlite. Water moderately during summer, less in winter. Prefers a humid but airy atmosphere (51°F in spring and summer); spray foliage in summer on hot days. Propagate by taking 3–4in (7.5–10cm) long cuttings of mature (leafy) stems in summer and root in warmth (65°F).

IVIES

IVIES ARE THE BEST PLANTS FOR FRAMED TOPIARY WORK. THEIR ATTRACTIVE EVERGREEN FOLIAGE COMES IN A WIDE RANGE OF SHAPES, SIZES, AND TEXTURES BOTH PLAIN LEAFED AND VARIEGATED. IVIES HAVE PLIABLE STEMS WHICH MAKE TRAINING VERY EASY.

BELOW
'Baby Face': green, new growth pale green, a good contrast to the dark, mature five-lobed leaves. Small and compact with a dense mass of small leaves.

ABOVE
'Duckfoot': green, three-lobed like a duck's webbed foot. Small, bushy growth.

RIGHT
'William Kennedy': white-gray, marbled leaves, narrowly edged with white, three-lobed with blunt, rounded ends and center lobe protruding furthest. Small or miniature in size, very dense bushy growth.

Almost any small- to medium-leafed ivy can be used for topiary, including the common, dark green-leafed *Hedera helix* which grows in hedgerows. However, some varieties are especially reliable. All the plants below are recommended for the purpose and are probably the best to experiment with if you have not tried this kind of topiary before. Plants have been selected for their dense, bushy growth, for being short-jointed (short pieces of stem between the side branches) and for branching readily without needing to pinch out the tips regularly.

LEFT
'Ivalace': green, five-lobed with distinctive wavy-edged, lacy leaves.

RIGHT
'Très Coupé (syn: 'Heraut,' 'Mini Heron'): green, narrow, deeply cut, five-lobed leaves with center lobe extending furthest. 'Sagittifolia' is similar. Small, very short-jointed stems, making a dense, bushy plant.

LEFT
'Direktor Badke': green, unusual rounded leaves. Very hardy, trailing growth.

KEY

deciduous

semi-evergreen

evergreen

flowering period months

patio

HYDRANGEA PANICULATA

Minimum temperature **–30°F/–34°C**
Zones **4–8**

Uses Flowering standards.
Characteristics Flowering shrub with green foliage producing very large, long-lasting, cone-shaped white or pink-flushed flower heads in late summer. Good varieties include 'Grandiflora' and 'Unique,' both of which turn from white to pinky-red in fall, and the white-flowered 'Floribunda' with elegant, tapering heads.
3–4ft (90–120cm) stem
Training Train as a standard, and once established, prune head hard back in spring to maintain shape and encourage large flowers.
Cultivation Grow in humus-rich soil. In pots, use potting soil blended with a proportion of soil-less mix. Keep well fed and watered. The minimum temperature tolerance depends on the variety. Propagate by softwood cuttings in summer.

ILEX
(Holly)

Minimum temperature **–10°F/–25°C** Zone **5**

Uses Traditional topiary, standards.
Characteristics Evergreen shrubs and trees, densely clothed in leathery, often prickly foliage that is dark green, gold or white/cream variegated. Female varieties produce red, orange or yellow berries usually only when there is a male plant nearby. Good variegated forms for topiary include popular varieties like *Ilex aquifolium* 'Golden Queen' (male), 'Handsworth New Silver' (female) and 'Silver Queen' (male) as well as *I.* x *altaclerensis* 'Golden King' (female). For plain, glossy green foliage and reliable fruit try *I. aquifolium* 'J.C. van Tol.'
Large standards with stems at least 5ft (1.5m) tall
Training Clip to shape with pruning shears.
Cultivation Grow in potting soil. Water container-grown plants freely during spring and summer. Propagate by semi-ripe cuttings in early summer.

JASMINUM POLYANTHUM
(Jasmine)

Minimum temperature **40°F/5°C** Zone **10**

Uses Covered frames.
Characteristics Greenhouse twiner/scrambler with dark green, pinnate leaves and white headily scented flowers that are pink in bud.
5–10ft (1.5–3m) tall, but much less in pots
Training Gently wind shoots around the frame and tie in place if necessary.
Cultivation Grow in potting soil. Keep soil moist at all times, but do not overwater. Spray leaves frequently. Keeping at a minimum temperature of 50–55°C promotes earlier flowering. Standing outdoors in light shade in summer is beneficial. Propagate by taking semi-ripe heel cuttings in summer and rooting in a heated propagator (62°F).
The hardy *Jasminum* x *stephanense* with yellow mottled leaves and pink blooms in summer is also suitable for training on a frame.

LAMIUM MACULATUM
(Dead nettle)

Minimum temperature **-30˚F/-34˚C** Zone **4**

Uses Moss-filled frames.

Characteristics Carpeting plants with silvery-white foliage and whorls of hooded, white or pink flowers in late spring and early summer. Good varieties include *L.m. roseum* and 'Pink Pewter,' with pale pink flowers, 'White Nancy' with white flowers and *L.m. album* 'Beacon Silver' which has cerise-pink blooms.
8 × 36in (20 × 90cm)

Training Pin down shoots to cover frame as they grow. Trim close to frame after flowering to maintain dense leaf cover.

Cultivation Grow in moisture-retentive but well-drained potting soil such as for hanging baskets. Do not allow to dry out in summer, but keep slightly drier in winter, because plants may suffer if exposed to excessive winter wet. Propagate by division in fall or stem tip cuttings in summer.

LANTANA CAMARA

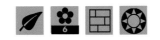

Minimum temperature **20˚F/-8˚C** Zone **9**

Uses Flowering standards.

Characteristics Bushy plants with deep green, crinkled foliage that smells unpleasant when rubbed. Clusters of small, verbena-like flowers often with several colors in the same head – a blend of red, orange, pink, mauve and yellow. There are also pure yellow, pure white, red-orange and pinky-mauve colored varieties. The flowers are highly attractive to butterflies, which seek their nectar. Spherical berries sometimes form after flowering. Good varieties for flowering standards include 'Mr Bessieres' (reddish-pink and yellow) and 'Snow White'.
1–4ft (30–120cm) × 1–3ft (30–90cm)

Training Prune head of standard hard back in late winter.

Cultivation Grow in well-drained, humus-rich potting soil of soil-less mix. Increase temperature to 50–55˚F at the start of the growing season. If grown in a greenhouse, provide a humid, well-ventilated atmosphere during the summer. Standards should be staked in windy gardens as the stems are very brittle. Keep a replacement set of plants growing to replace old and twiggy specimens. Propagate by taking 3in (7.5cm) long shoot tip cuttings in summer and rooting in a heated propagator.

HOLLIES

HOLLIES ARE FIRST-RATE TOPIARY PLANTS. THERE ARE BRIGHTLY VARIEGATED FORMS TO MAKE THE WINTER GARDEN SPARKLE AND FEMALE VARIETIES OFFER THE ADDED BONUS OF BERRIES IN RED, ORANGE, OR YELLOW. HOLLIES MAY BE TRAINED INTO A VARIETY OF SIMPLE SHAPES AND MAKE EXCELLENT LARGE STANDARDS.

RIGHT
*Trained as a standard, the variety '**Handsworth New Silver**' can be grown in large tubs for the terrace or planted in the border to add height and a touch of formality.*

LEFT
Ilex aquifolium *'Silver Queen' is a male variety which has blackish-purple shoots and dark green leaves, faintly marbled with gray and bordered by creamy-white. Choose a young, single-stemmed specimen like this to train a standard.*

Left to their own devices, they will often produce a cone-shaped outline, a pattern which can be further emphasized by judicious pruning. Hollies are tough, forgiving plants and like yew will resprout from old wood when hard pruned, making it possible to reshape existing plants in the garden. Unlike many evergreen shrubs which are highly vulnerable to cold winter winds, established hollies, especially varieties of the common holly, *Ilex aquifolium*, withstand a fair amount of exposure, so they are useful where bay, for example, would be too tender to contemplate. Hollies are either male or female, so if you want a good crop of berries, check that you have a female variety (the cultivar names are not a reliable indication of sex!). You'll also need a nearby male plant, for example, *Ilex aquifolium* 'Golden Queen' or 'Golden Milkboy' to provide the pollen.

RIGHT
Ilex x altaclerensis
'Golden King' is, in fact, a female variety, and will produce red berries if a male is growing nearby. This is a somewhat less prickly variety than most and the bright variegation makes it a popular choice.

RIGHT
Ilex aquifolium *'J.C. Van Tol' is a useful variety if you want holly berries but don't have a nearby male - it produces a profusion of scarlet fruits all by itself! The glossy deep green foliage is virtually spineless.*

LAURUS NOBILIS
(Sweet bay)

Minimum temperature **20°F/-5°C** Zone **8**

Uses Traditional topiary, standards.

Characteristics Culinary herb with leathery, deep green leaves, making large shrubs or small trees in favorable areas. Shelter from cold winter winds. In exposed parts of the country provide extra winter protection. Small, pale yellow flowers appear in spring, followed by small black fruits. Standards with 3–4ft (90–120cm) stems can be raised relatively quickly.

Training Clip to shape in summer using pruning shears to avoid damaging leaves. An additional trim in late spring may also be necessary to maintain a good outline.

Cultivation Grow in well-drained potting soil. In winter, insulate pots or, in the North, move plants into a greenhouse for added protection. Propagate by semi-ripe cuttings at midsummer.

LIGUSTRUM OVALIFOLIUM
(Privet)

Minimum temperature **-10°F/-25°C** Zone **6**

Uses Traditional topiary.

Characteristics Common hedging plant with small, oval-shaped leaves that are plain green, gold-variegated ('Aureum') or white-variegated ('Argenteum'). Small plumes of white flowers appear in midsummer on the previous year's growth. In very cold winters, plants lose their leaves.

12 × 10ft (3.5 × 3m)

Training Clip to shape in mid-spring.

Cultivation Dislikes poor, thin, alkaline soils. Water freely. Propagate by semi-ripe cuttings in late spring/early summer or by hardwood cuttings in winter.

LONICERA NITIDA
(Boxleaf honeysuckle, Poor man's box)

Minimum temperature **0°F/-10°C** Zone **7**

Uses Traditional topiary, standards.

Characteristics Dense, twiggy shrubs with very small evergreen or semi-evergreen leaves in plain green or golden-yellow (the less vigorous 'Baggessen's Gold'). Insignificant, tiny creamy-white flowers in late spring are sometimes followed by purple berries.

5 × 12ft (1.5 × 3.5m)

Training Clip to shape in spring using shears and remove winter damage.

Cultivation Avoid poor, thin soils and either dry or waterlogged sites. Plants may lose leaves if exposed to strong, cold winds. Strong sunlight may scorch variegated plants. Easily roots from semi-ripe cuttings in late summer.

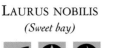

LONICERA PERICLYMENUM
(Common honeysuckle, Woodbine)

Minimum temperature **–20°F/–28°C** Zone **5**

Uses Flowering standards.

Characteristics Twining climbers with long, pliable stems covered in large green or reddish-green, oval leaves. Flower clusters heavily scented. 'Belgica' (early Dutch honeysuckle) flowers in early summer with purple, red and yellow blooms and reddish-green foliage. 'Serotina' (late Durch honeysuckle) flowers early fall with red-purple and cream blooms. Both varieties sometimes produce glistening red berries in clusters in early fall.

4–5ft (120–150cm) stem

Training Follow instructions for Training a Climber into a Standard, page 56, using several stems twisted around the stake to form the trunk. Alternatively, train shoots up into a purchased globe-headed frame. Once established, prune away some of the shoots older than about three years from the head in early spring to maintain vigor.

Cultivation Avoid dry sites as this makes plants susceptible to mildew: rich, moisture-retentive soil is best. Honeysuckles sometimes suffer bad attacks from aphids which, if not treated early on, will cause the leaves to become distorted. Keep a watch in spring and give a strong spray of water or treat with pyrethrum before numbers increase dramatically. Propagate by semi-ripe cuttings in early summer.

MAGNOLIA X SOULANGEANA
(Saucer magnolia)

Minimum temperature **–30°F/–32°C** Zone **4**

Uses Flowering standards.

Characteristics Large, goblet-shaped flowers of very light pink with purple shading at the petal base. The flowers are produced before the green leaves emerge.

5ft (150cm) stem

Training After training, prune lightly to maintain a well-shaped head without reducing the flowering.

Cultivation Avoid very dry or alkaline soils. Keep moist at all times during the growing season, but avoid waterlogged conditions. Find a site away from the early morning sun, which can damage frosted blooms. Propagation is difficult, but try layering or semi-ripe cuttings in early summer.

KEY

deciduous

semi-evergreen

evergreen

flowering
period
months

patio

MYRTUS COMMUNIS
(Myrtle)

Minimum temperature **20°F/–5°C** Zone **9**

Uses Traditional topiary, standards.

Characteristics Aromatic, evergreen shrub with dense, fine, deep green foliage. White flowers with central boss of fluffy stamens produced in mid to late summer. Commonly grown as a large container plant and overwintered indoors or in a greenhouse, if possible.
6 × 6ft (3.5 × 3.5m)

Training Clip with shears in early spring to maintain shape and remove frost-damaged shoots from plants grown outdoors.

Cultivation Grow in well-drained potting soil. A sheltered site is best. Propagate by semi-ripe cuttings in early summer.

NERIUM OLEANDER
(Oleander)

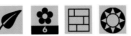

Minimum temperature **50°F/10°C** Zone **10**

Uses Flowering standards.

Characteristics Evergreen shrub with long, pointed leathery leaves and periwinkle-shaped flowers in a range of colors. Very long flowering period. All parts of the plant are poisonous.
3–4ft (90–120cm) tall stem

Training Maintain a compact head by annual pruning – cut flowering shoots back by half after flowering and prune lateral shoots to 4in (10cm).

Cultivation Grow in potting soil. Avoid waterlogging, but keep container-grown plants well watered during the growing season. Water carefully in winter. Propagate by semi-ripe cuttings in summer.

NERTERA GRANDENSIS
(Bead plant)

Minimum temperature **20°F/–6°C** Zone **9**

Uses Moss-filled frames.

Characteristics Creeping perennial plant grown as an annual in the Southwest. Mid-green foliage, greenish insignificant flowers; bright orange berries in summer and fall lasting for many weeks.
½ × 4in (1 × 10cm)

Training None needed.

Cultivation Grow in moisture-retentive potting soil that is also free-draining and gritty enough to prevent waterlogging. Benefits from standing outdoors in summer, but keep in a sheltered, shaded place to prevent drying out. Propagate by division in spring or shoot tip cuttings.

PAROCHETUS COMMUNIS
(Shamrock Pea)

Minimum temperature **32°F/0°C** Zone **10**

Uses Moss-filled frames.

Characteristics This member of the pea family can be grown in hanging baskets in summer. It roots where its runners touch the soil and is therefore ideal for covering stuffed framed topiary. Brilliant blue pea flowers are carried over clover-like leaves. When the plant is growing actively, they bloom almost continually.

1–2in (2.5–5cm) tall, spread indefinite

Training Pin runners into position until they root.

Cultivation Grow in gritty, moisture-retentive soil. Give moderate shade on a patio. Keep in a cool, airy environment when in a greenhouse. Propagate by separating off rooted runners at any time of year.

PASSIFLORA CAERULEA
(Common passion flower)

Minimum temperature **0°F/–18°C** Zone **7**

Uses Covered frames.

Characteristics Fast-growing climber that clings to its supports by means of tendrils. Palmate leaves divided into five narrow, green leaflets. Complex and exotic-looking, white flowers with blue and purple markings, sometimes followed by egg-shaped yellow fruits. Other species and varieties are available from specialist growers, with spectacular red, blue, purple or white flowers. These all require higher overwintering temperatures than the common passion flower.

30ft (10m) tall, less in a pot

Training Large pot-grown plants trained onto a trellis are sometimes available, but because of the tendrils, the stems are very difficult to untangle and dislodge for re-training. Start with a young, untrained plant. Cut away any over-vigorous or excess growth in February/March and trim side shoots to 6in (15cm) to keep plant within bounds.

Cultivation Grow in well-drained potting soil. Water copiously during summer, less in winter. Provide light shade if in a greenhouse during summer. Propagate from seed in a heated propagator or from 3–4in (7.5–10cm) long stem cuttings rooted in a heated propagator.

KEY

deciduous

semi-evergreen

evergreen

**flowering
period
months**

patio

PELARGONIUM
(Geranium)

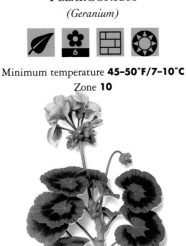

Minimum temperature **45–50°F/7–10°C**
Zone **10**

Uses Flowering standards.

Characteristics Geraniums are familiar tender perennials with lobed leaves that are either plain green or attractively banded with bronze, maroon, creamy-white, gold, pink, or red. The foliage is pungent-smelling when brushed against. Showy flowers in dome-shaped heads are produced over a very long period. Many shades available from white and soft pastels to vibrant oranges, reds, pinks, and purple. Some of the more vigorous scented-leaf geraniums, which smell of lemon, apple, mint, or rose may also be used, but the flowers are not as well developed.

Untrained plants may eventually reach up to 6ft (1.8m) but standards with 2–3ft long stems are more usual

Training Start standards with cuttings taken in summer. Grow these on through the winter pinching out all side shoots up to the top three or four leaves. When the desired stem height has been reached, pinch out the tip to promote branching of the head. Continue to pinch out the side shoots when they have reached the three- or four-leaf stage.

Cultivation Grow in well-drained potting soil. Avoid overwatering, which promotes stem rot. Keep barely moist through winter. If grown under glass in summer, provide light shade, ventilate well and try to keep temperatures at 55°C or below. Propagate by taking cuttings using 3in (7.5cm) long shoot tips and rooting in a pot of moist, but not wet, multi-purpose mix or potting and cutting soil. Leave pots uncovered in a warm, light place and pot cuttings individually when rooted.

PRUNUS LUSITANICA
(Portugal Laurel)

Minimum temperature **0°F/–18°C**
Zone **7**

Uses Traditional topiary, standards.

Characteristics Dark green, glossy-leaved shrub, sometimes used for hedging. Spikes of white-scented flowers in early summer. *Prunus laurocerasus* (cherry laurel) can also be used to make round-headed standards quickly, but the much larger leaves make it unsuitable for shaping into more intricate forms. Vigorous, may be trained to have a 4–6ft (120–180cm) high stem.

Training May be cut back hard as the plant recovers well. Shape in late summer, using pruning shears to avoid unsightly cut edges to the leaves.

Cultivation Grow in humus-rich loam. Propagate by semi-ripe cuttings taken in early summer.

PYRACANTHA
(Firethorn)

Minimum temperature **–10°F/–24°C** Zone **6**

Uses Traditional topiary.

Characteristics Tough evergreen or semi-evergreen wall shrub or hedging plant with small, deep green, glossy leaves on dense, twiggy, thorny growth. Creamy-white flowers in early summer. The long-lasting berries in late summer/fall are a major feature. For healthy, vigorous growth and orange-red berries choose 'Orange Glow.' 8 × 8ft (2.5 × 2.5m); standards on 4 ft (120cm) stems are ideal

Training Clip to shape in summer. The harder you prune for formal shaping, the less flowers and therefore berries will form.

Cultivation Grow in potting soil; avoid extreme alkalinity. Drought-tolerant, but water plants in pots well during fruit formation. Propagate by semi-ripe cuttings in early summer.

RHODOCHITON ATROSANGUINEUS
(Purple Bell Vine)

Minimum temperature **32°F/0°C** Zone **10**

Uses Covered frames, moss-filled frames.

Characteristics Slender-stemmed climber with pointed, heart-shaped leaves and curious hanging flowers of red and deep purple. Normally grown as a greenhouse plant, but may be grown in very sheltered spots outside in the summer as an annual or as a temporary house plant.

Over a number of years it may reach 5ft (1.5m), but in its first year from seed, 2½ft (75cm) is more likely

Training Guide the stems over the frame as it grows and pin shoots down into the moss as necessary.

Cultivation Grow from seed sown in early spring in a heated propagator. For long-term plantings, grow in good potting soil. Otherwise, a soil-less mix is fine.

RHOICISSUS RHOMBOIDEA
(African grape)

Minimum temperature **45°F/7°C** Zone **10**

Uses Covered frames.

Characteristics Vigorous climber with glossy dark green, tooth-edged leaflets arranged in threes. Tiny grape-like clusters of fruit occasionally produced, hence the common name.

Up to 8ft (20m) tall

Training Tie shoots onto frame using soft twine so as not to damage them.

Cultivation Grow in potting soil or soil-less mix. Propagate by stem cuttings during spring and summer.

ROSMARINUS OFFICINALIS
(Rosemary)

Minimum temperature **20°** to **10°F/ –5°** to **–12°C** Zones **8–9**

Uses Covered frames, standards.

Characteristics Aromatic, woody herb with gray-green, needle-like leaves and many small-lipped flowers. Flowers are pale mauve-blue in the species and common forms. The main flowering period is in the spring, but there are often intermittent flowers until fall. Upright and prostrate varieties available, some more tender than others and benefiting from winter protection such as a cool greenhouse or pot insulation (see page 71). Plants may eventually become too woody and sparse, but can be cut back in spring and trained again using the re-growth.

Recommended varieties are: *R. officinalis* 'Prostratus' (a prostrate form only 1ft/30cm high); 'Miss Jessopp's Upright' (strongly upright form); 'Benenden Blue' (smaller growing than average, gentian-blue flowers); *R.o.* 'Roseus' (lilac-pink flowers); 'Severn Sea' (deep blue, free-flowering but less hardy than the species); *R.o. albiflorus* (white). 4 × 5ft (120 × 150cm)

Training Tie new shoots to frames as they grow and pinch out tips to encourage bushy growth. Clip formal topiary in spring. To prevent the heads of established standards from becoming thin and woody, remove about one-third of the oldest shoots every year in spring.

Cultivation Grow in well-drained, gritty, potting soil. Cactus soil with perlite added is suitable. Do not overwater, but do not let plants dry out, either. Propagate by rooting 5in (13cm) long basal or heeled cuttings in cold frame in late summer.

SEDUM
(Stonecrop)

Minimum temperature **–20°F/–28°C** Zone **5**

Uses Moss-filled frames.

Characteristics Vigorous groundcovers with succulent green, gray or in some varieties silver-white, pink- or purple-flushed leaves. Clusters of tiny, star-shaped yellow, pink or purple flowers are produced at different times during the summer according to species and may be removed with fine, sharp scissors to maintain a smooth appearance. Good, readily available varieties include *S. spathulifolium* with pinkish-gray leaves, and *S.s.* 'Cape Blanco' with blue-gray foliage and *S. acre* with green leaves and yellow flowers. 1–4 × 8–15in (2.5–10 × 20–37.5cm) depending on variety

Training Pin stray shoots into position to cover the frame.

Cultivation Grow in well-drained potting soil. Propagate by division.

SEMPERVIVUM
(Hens-and-chicks, houseleek)

Minimum temperature **-20°F/-28°C** Zone **5**

Uses Moss-filled frames.

Characteristics Rosette-forming plant that spreads by surrounding itself with little offsets. Succulent leaves in a variety of colors from green to purple-red. Some appear almost white due to a dense covering of hair. The flowers are rose-red. Many varieties, but the cobweb houseleek, *S. arachnoïdeum* is one of the most commonly grown. Hardiness varies according to species.
½–1 × 12in (1.25–2.5 × 30cm)

Training None required. Remove flower spikes as they form.

Cultivation Grow in well-drained potting soil. Propagate by detaching rooted offsets in fall or spring.

SOLEIROLIA SOLEIROLII, SYN. HELXINE
(Baby's tears, Mind-your-own-business)

Minimum temperature **20°F/–5°C** Zone **9**

Uses Moss-filled frames.

Characteristics Carpeting plant making low mounds of tiny leaves. Where it is hardy, the plain green-leaved variety grows flat outside like moss covering damp stonework and soil. Foliage is mid-green, but pale lime green and pale gray-green varieties are available.

Training Little needed. Trim errant shoots.

Cultivation Any good potting soil will do, provided it's moisture-retentive. Keep soil constantly moist in summer, reduce watering in winter and avoid waterlogging. Spray frequently and maintain a humid atmosphere. If grown on a patio, keep topiary in a sheltered, semi-shaded spot to prevent drying out. Keep cool indoors, below 72°F in summer, ideally 38–42°F in winter. Propagate by gently pulling off rooted chunks or individual stems and potting up.

STEPHANOTIS FLORIBUNDA
(Madagascar jasmine)

Minimum temperature **55°F/13°C** Zone **10**

Uses Covered frames.

Characteristics Twining plant with succulent, glossy green foliage and waxy, heavily scented white flowers. Up to 10ft (3m) tall.

Training Wind the stem around the frame as it grows.

Cultivation Grow in a potting soil or soil-less mix. Stephanotis dislikes large fluctuations in temperature. Allow the soil to dry out a little between waterings and water sparingly in winter. Spray foliage frequently in summer. Propagate from root cuttings taken from 4in (10cm) long, non-flowering side shoots during summer; grow in a heated propagator.

deciduous

semi-evergreen

evergreen

flowering
period
months

patio

SYRINGA VULGARIS
(Lilac)

Minimum temperature **-40°F/-40°C** Zone **3**

Uses Flowering standards.

Characteristics Shrub or small tree with sweetly scented, cone-shaped clusters of flowers in early summer. Double- and single-flowered varieties are available mainly in shades of purple, but also pink, red, white and pale yellow. Large heart-shaped, mid-green leaves. Lilacs have a tendency to develop suckers and may get too large for some gardens unless trained as standards. 4–5ft (120–150cm) stems

Training Remove faded flowers. Pinch out shoot tips or prune lightly to control size and shape of head immediately after flowering. Cut out weak and crossing branches from fall onwards.

Cultivation Grow in potting soil – lilacs prefer alkaline soil. Avoid waterlogging. Propagate by softwood cuttings in summer.

TAXUS BACCATA
(English yew)

Minimum temperature **-10°F/-22°C** Zone **6**

Uses Covered frames, traditional topiary, standards.

Characteristics Dense, upright-growing conifer with dark green or gold, needle-like leaves traditionally used for topiary. Female plants produce poisonous red berries. 15 × 15ft (4.5 × 4.5m)

Training Prune at any time.

Cultivation Grow in potting soil – English yew grows well on alkaline as well as slightly acid soil. In the garden it prefers moist, well-drained conditions. Propagate from seed or heel cuttings in early fall.

THYMUS
(Thyme)

Minimum temperature **20°** to **10°F/**
-5° to **-15°C** Zones **7-9**

Uses Moss-filled frames, standards.

Characteristics Creeping aromatic herb with many species and varieties from completely prostrate to mound-forming plants in shades of green and also gold-variegated. The tiny flowers in pink, purple or white, are a magnet for bees. Good dense mat-forming varieties include *T. praecox* and *T. serpyllum coccineus* with cerise-pink flowers. For standards, choose bushy upright varieties like the lemon-scented *T. × citrodorus* 'Silver Queen.'
2½ × 8–12in (6 × 20–30cm)

Training Pin shoots down to cover frame. If areas die out, remove dead material and replant through the mesh.

Cultivation Grow in potting soil. Winter wet may cause rotting, so some shelter from rain is advisable. Propagate by division in summer or by 2in (5cm) long heel cuttings in midsummer.

TRACHELOSPERMUM JASMINOÏDES
(Star jasmine, Confederate jasmine)

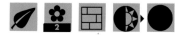

Minimum temperature **10°F/-12°C** Zone **8**

Uses Covered frames.

Characteristics Climber suitable for an unheated greenhouse, grown outdoors in the South. The white or cream flowers are periwinkle-shaped and very fragrant; the green leaves are small and leathery. *T. asiaticum* is similar and *T. jasminoïdes* 'Variegatum' has cream-edged foliage. 10–12ft (3–3.5m) tall or more

Training Wind stems around frame.

Cultivation Grow in potting soil with some soil-less mix added. Will survive temperatures of 10°F if the pot is well-insulated but best to move indoors to a greenhouse for the winter where hardiness is questionable. Propagate by semi-ripe cuttings during late summer or fall.

VIBURNUM TINUS
(Laurustinus)

Minimum temperature **10°F/-12°C** Zone **8**

Uses Flowering standards, traditional topiary.

Characteristics Evergreen shrub with dense, deep green foliage and compact growth. Dome-shaped clusters of honey-scented, white, sometimes pink-tinged, flowers open over a long period. The flower buds are pink. 3–4ft (80–120cm) stem

Training Remove winter-damaged shoots in early summer and pinch out shoot tips to maintain dense, bushy growth.

Cultivation Grow in moisture-retentive potting soil. Do not allow plants grown in containers to dry out. Propagate by semi-ripe cuttings in early fall.

VITIS
(Grape)

Minimum temperature **-20°C/-28°C** Zone **5**

Uses Fruiting standards.

Characteristics Vigorous vines climbing by tendrils with large, green palmate leaves. Many grape species and varieties are available. Some are more suitable for growing as standards than others, and take up a lot less space and are easier to manage. The fruit ripens well in the warmth of a greenhouse. Hardiness varies according to variety. Some are only suitable for indoor cultivation. 3–4ft (90–120cm) stem

Training See page 62.

Cultivation Grow in potting soil. Light shade if grown in a greenhouse in summer. Propagate by hardwood cuttings in late fall.

Training See page 62.

KEY

full sun

light shade

moderate shade

three quarter shade

full shade

KEY

deciduous

semi-evergreen

evergreen

flowering
period
months

patio

VITIS VINIFERA 'PURPUREA'
(Purple-leaved grapevine)

Minimum temperature **–10°F/–24°C** Zone **6**

Uses Standards.

Characteristics Purple-leaved variety of the common wine grape that is grown for its ornamental foliage and red fall color. Fruit like mini-bunches of grapes, purple with a blue bloom.

3–4ft (90–120cm) stem

Training See page 61.

Cultivation Grow in potting soil. Do not allow to dry out. Propagate by semi-ripe cuttings in early summer.

WISTERIA FLORIBUNDA
(Japanese wisteria)

Minimum temperature **–20°F/–28°C** Zone **5**

Uses Flowering standards.

Characteristics Vigorous flowering climber that requires pruning to keep its size in check and promote flowering. Large green pinnate leaves and long cascading tassels of fragrant pea-like flowers in purple, pink, or white depending on variety. Select named, grafted varieties as otherwise plants may not flower. Avoid cold, exposed positions as flower buds are vulnerable to damage.

4ft (120cm) stem

Training See page 59.

Cultivation Grow in rich, moisture-retentive potting soil. Propagation is difficult – it is best to buy commercially grafted plants.

USING THE ZONE MAP

Zones are indicated in the Directory for each of the plants. These relate to the areas indicated on the map. The temperatures given indicate the lowest range that a plant will tolerate. But remember that this is a guide only, and the conditions that a plant will tolerate depend on many factors, such as the amount of shelter given to the plant and its position within your garden.

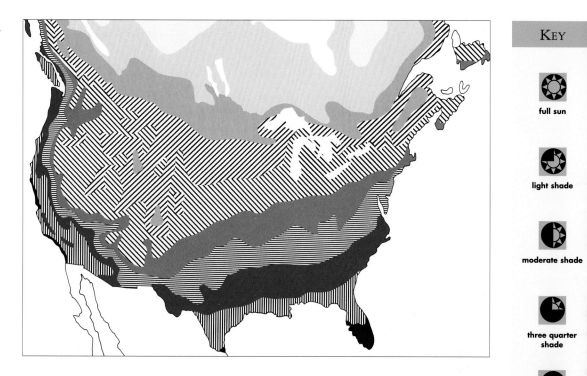

KEY

full sun

light shade

moderate shade

three quarter shade

full shade

KEY
AVERAGE ANNUAL MINIMUM TEMPERATURE

Zone 1	Below -50°F	Below -45°C
Zone 2	-50°F to -40°F	-45°C to -40°C
Zone 3	-40°F to -30°F	-40°C to -34°C
Zone 4	-30°F to -20°F	-34°C to -29°C
Zone 5	-20°F to -10°F	-29°C to -23°C
Zone 6	-10°F to 0°F	-23°C to -17°C
Zone 7	0°F to 10°F	-17°C to 12°C
Zone 8	10°F to 20°F	-12°C to -7°C
Zone 9	20°F to 30°F	-7°C to -1°C
Zone 10	30°F to 40°F	-1°C to 5°C

ADDRESSES OF SUPPLIERS

All of the companies listed here supply by mail order.

Key~

(P) ~ plants suitable for topiary
(T) ~ ready-made topiary
(F) ~ topiary frames

ANDREW CRACE DESIGNS
131 Bourne Lane
Much Hadham
Herts SG10 6ER
England
Tel: (01279) 842685
(F)

AVANT GARDEN
77 Ledbury Road
London W11 2AG
England
Tel: (0171) 229 4408
(F)

BOSMERE PRODUCTS LTD
189 Victoria Road North
Portsmouth
Hampshire PO5 1AJ
England
Tel: (01705) 863541
(F)

BOSMERE INC.
P.O. Box 363
323 Corban Avenue S.W.
Concord N.C. 28026
USA
Tel: (704) 784 1608

CAPITAL GARDEN PRODUCTS
Gibbs Reed Barn
Ticehurst
East Sussex TN5 7HE
England
Tel: (01580) 201092
(F)

ENGLISH HURDLE
Curload
Stoke St. Gregory
Taunton, Somerset TA3 6JD
England
Tel: (01823) 698418
(F)

FIBREX NURSERIES LTD
Honeybourne Road
Tabworth
Stratford-on-Avon
Warwickshire
CV 378XT
England
Tel: (01789) 720788
(P)

LANGLEY BOXWOOD NURSERY
Rake
Nr Liss
Hampshire GU33 7JL
England
Tel: (01730) 894467
(P) (T)

PHOEBE'S GARDEN CENTRE
2 Penerley Road
London SE6 2LQ
England
Tel: (0181) 698 4365
(P)

RAYMENT WIREWORK
The Forge
Durlock, Minster
Thanet
Kent CT12 4HE
England
Tel: (01843) 821628
(F)

READS NURSERY
Hales Hall
Loddon
Norfolk NR14 6QW
England
Tel: (01508) 548395
(P) (T)

THE ROMANTIC GARDEN
Swannington
Norwich
Norfolk NR9 5NW
England
Tel: (01603) 261488
(P) (T) (F)

THE SECRET GARDEN
Westow Street
Upper Norwood
London SE19 3AF
England
Tel: (0181) 771 8200

SECRET GARDEN TOPIAR-EASE
P.O. Box 25
Morpeth
Northumberland NE65 7XA
England
Tel: (01669) 620941
(F)

TERRACE & GARDEN LTD
Orchard House
Patmore End
Ugley
Bishop's Stortford
Herts CM22 6JA
England
Tel: (01799) 543289
(F)

TOPIARY INC.
41 Bering Street
Tampa
Florida 33606
USA
Tel: (813) 837 2841
(F)

WADHAM TRADING COMPANY
Wadham House
Southrop
Nr Lechlade
Gloucestershire GL7 3PB
England
Tel: (01367) 850499
(F)

INDEX

ACKNOWLEDGEMENTS

QUARTO would like to thank the following for allowing us to reproduce
photographs used in this book.

Key~ *a* above, *b* below, *l* left, *r* right

Garden Matters *6ar*, 80; Andrew Lawson *9a*; S & O Mathews *6b*; Jackie Newey *9b*, 67, 77;
Howard Rice *14r*, *78b*; Secret Garden Topiar-Ease 8, 24, *45a*, 72, *74bl*, *79b*, *87al*, *bl*, & *br*,
89al; Harry Smith Horticultural Collection *7ar* & *br*, *11l*, 44, *79a*.

All other photographs are the copyright of Quarto Publishing.

Quarto would like to thank *Carole Guyton* at *Topiary, Inc* for kindly supplying the following
frames used in the book: swan, pages 34 & 33, heart pages 69 & 84, cats page78,
candle cone and angel,page 86, Teddy "Roosevelt" page *87r*; *Andrew Crace* for supplying the frames
shown on pages 81, *82bl* & *ar*, *83b*; and *Terrace & Garden Ltd*, for supplying the
frame shown on page 73. Other frames were supplied and planted by *Joan Clifton* at *Avant Garden*;
Reads Nursery; *The Romantic Garden*; and *The Secret Garden*.

We would like to thank *Giles Blunden* of *Blundens Wireworks*, who made the frames shown on pages
16-23, and *Stephen Crisp* who supplied plant sprigs used in the book's Directory section.

We are grateful to *The Secret Garden* who kindly supplied some of the fuchsias and hollies
shown on pages 102-3 and 110-11 and some of the standards on pages 56-7 and page 88;
and *Phoebe's Garden Centre* supplied the tools and equipment used in photography.

Finally, a special thank you to
Jill Swinney at *Secret Garden Topiar-Ease*
for her contribution to this book.